Sensing
His Presence

Hearing
His Voice

Sensing His Presence

Hearing His Voice

HOW TO CULTIVATE HEARING THE Voice of God

CARROL JOHNSON SHEWMAKE

REVIEW AND HERALD® PUBLISHING ASSOCIATION
HAGERSTOWN, MD 21740

The author assumes full responsibility for the accuracy of all facts and
quotations as cited in this book.

Unless otherwise noted, Bible texts are from the *Holy Bible, New
International Version.* Copyright © 1973, 1978, 1984, International Bible
Society. Used by permission of Zondervan Bible Publishers.

Texts credited to NEB are from *The New English Bible.* © The Delegates of
the Oxford University Press and the Syndics of the Cambridge University
Press 1961, 1970. Reprinted by permission.

Texts credited to NKJV are from The New King James Version. Copyright ©
1979, 1980, 1982, Thomas Nelson, Inc., Publishers.

Bible texts credited to TEV are from the *Good News Bible*—Old Testament:
Copyright © American Bible Society 1976; New Testament: Copyright ©
American Bible Society 1966, 1971, 1976.

Verses marked TLB are taken from *The Living Bible,* copyright © 1971 by
Tyndale House Publishers, Wheaton, Ill. Used by permission.

This book was
Edited by Gerald Wheeler
Cover design by Helcio Deslandes
Typeset: 11/13 Optima

PRINTED IN U.S.A.

98 97 96 95 94   10 9 8 7 6 5 4 3 2 1

R & H Cataloging Service
Shewmake, Carrol Johnson, 1927–
    Sensing His presence, hearing His voice.

    1. Christian life. 2. God—Knowableness.
I. Title.
                    248.2

ISBN 0-8280-0829-9

Contents

Grandpa Abraham's Story

For years I puzzled over the stories of my great-great-great-grandfather (by adoption, I suspect—not by bloodlines) Abraham, and marveled. Oh, the earliest stories—how God led him to move away from the country that had been the family home for generations, and to wander as a nomad with his wife and retinue of servants, seeking a nebulous country God would someday give him—I could understand that part. I too have an adventurous spirit and would willingly search out the unknown path, the new city, the new job, new friends, new challenges—all following an inner voice.

No, the story that tried my heart over and over again had to do with the miracle son God gave to Grandpa Abraham and Grandma Sarah in their old age. I loved the account of his birth, and I laughed right along with Grandma Sarah as I rejoiced with her in her precious gift of a son. That wasn't the story that bothered me. No, it was a later incident—one that left out Grandma and centered on Grandpa.

You see, I am a mother myself, and I know that children are mighty precious in the eyes of their parents. So I just couldn't understand how in the world Grandpa Abraham could have *ever* believed that it was *God's* voice that asked him to offer his only son—the miracle boy—as a sacrifice. God doesn't ask people to kill—He gives life. The only problem I saw with my reasoning was that a careful reading of the Bible account (Gen. 22) showed that Grandpa Abraham was right—and I was wrong. It *was* God's voice speaking to him. Although God does not ask us to kill, yet He used this request as a test of Grandpa's faith. God never intended for him to kill his son. But God invited him to prove his willingness to follow God's directions faithfully even when he could not understand.

What bothered me most was the realization that I would not have passed that test. How in the world, I wondered, could a person be *sure* it was *God's* voice he or she was hearing? How did Grandpa Abraham *know* it was the Lord speaking? How could he have been sure enough to gather the wood, call his son, and start out on that dreadful expedition?

Often during the years of raising my children from birth through childhood and on into adolescence I wondered about

Abraham's faith and how he was able to so positively identify God's voice. My children were all teenagers when one day the answer to my question came to me in a flash.

Abraham recognized God's voice clearly *because he heard it every day. He was as familiar with God's voice as he was with Sarah's!* The patriarch had welcomed God in human form (unknowingly!) in his own tents. He had talked with Him face-to-face as he pleaded with God not to destroy the city of Sodom. Scripture describes Abraham as God's friend (2 Chron. 20:7; Isa. 41:8; James 2:23).

No, Abraham did not question but that it was God who told him to sacrifice his son. He *knew* beyond the shadow of a doubt who was speaking, for he knew God's familiar voice. Oh, I'm sure he asked Him for confirmation.

"God," I can imagine him saying, "is this really You? Would You tell me to sacrifice my son, as the heathen do their children? Why would You ask me to do this?"

But all the time Abraham knew that it was God who had spoken. He didn't know why the Lord requested him to do it—although he may have guessed that it had something to do with his past failures to trust God fully. But one thing Abraham had learned over his years of daily companionship with God—He had a reason for whatever He asked, and that it would somehow fit into a bright future. Trusting God fully, the old father *knew* that it was God who had spoken to him. Despite the fact that it seemed to contradict the divine promise to create a nation from Isaac's descendants, the patriarch *trusted* the God who had always proved faithful in the past.

In some way God would keep His promise and would be glorified through Abraham's obedience. Abraham's struggle was not in believing that it was God who had spoken to him—rather his struggle was in obeying God against his own desires. And perhaps obedience wasn't a struggle either at this time, for he had learned it the hard way by past experiences. I'm not implying that it was easy for Abraham to choose to offer up his son. It had to be agony. But obedience was the only possible path for him to take. Like Enoch, Abraham had been walking daily with God, ever drawing closer and closer to Him. To hear God speak, for Abraham, was to obey Him.

When I began to realize this, Grandpa Abraham's story lit up my life. I longed to be able to identify positively the divine voice in my own life. And so I began my pilgrimage of *learning to listen.*

CHAPTER ONE

"My Sheep Listen to My Voice"

*I*t's wise to be careful today about listening to voices. I am not speaking of audible ones heard with the human ear, but of inner voices perceived by the heart. God has designed only one avenue to commune with humanity—through the intricacies of the human mind. But He is not the only one with access to the brain. Other voices barrage the gateways to the senses as well.

And today the errant voices are louder, more numerous, more blatant, than ever before in history. In one way this is good, for their obviousness makes it easier than ever before to identify the voice of the enemy and avoid him. But wisdom enters into the picture only when we realize that unless armed with truth even the sincere may find themselves deceived. Some people, fearful of treading on the fringes of the New Age, determine not to listen to *any* internal voice at all. They accept only the written word of God and avoid anything that seems emotional. But that can be dangerous for at least two reasons:

One, unless we believe with the *heart,* an emotional response, we don't really believe. The story of the death of Jesus on the cross remains only a historical event until we see that it was our sins that put Him there. Faith is a heart response to truth. So it's impossible to believe with the intellect only.

Two, we cannot understand the Bible except as the Holy Spirit enlightens the mind. Satan himself quoted Scripture to Jesus to prove error. In fact, he is still doing that dastardly work.

Unless we have a personal relationship with Jesus through the Holy Spirit, we will listen to the wrong voice, sincerely believing it to be God's—for everyone hears and follows some voice.

Since the publication of my two books on prayer *(Practical Pointers to Personal Prayer* [Review and Herald Publishing Association, 1989] and *Sanctuary Secrets to Personal Prayer* [Review, 1990]), I have had the opportunity to speak to many people about God's great desire to have an intimate family relationship with every human being born into our world. I have seen the heart hunger in searching eyes, heard the hopelessness and despair in sad voices, and realize with sorrow that *the majority, even of Christians, do not have a sense of God's presence in their daily lives.* It is in answer to that lack that I am writing this book. I'd like to share some of the joy I find daily with Jesus, and give some practical pointers on how we can cultivate hearing the voice of God daily, both in prayer and throughout the day as we work, study, and play. This isn't something we have to persuade God to do reluctantly. Oh, no! Rather, it is God's will for each of us. He *is* speaking, but we just aren't listening— or don't have the confidence to believe that God is communicating to us personally.

Practice of the presence of God in my personal life is not something that has come naturally for me. I have often felt alone, sure that God has finally turned away from me in anger and disgust at my faithlessness and carelessness. But God has finally persuaded me that His promises are true and that He will *never, never, never* leave me or forsake me (Joshua 1:5). That knowledge has released me from the panic that always in the past accompanied my sense of aloneness, and it has given me freedom to put into practice a sense of the presence of God. I am able to trust God no matter how formidable my circumstances may seem. Because of this knowledge, I now view prayer in a totally different way than I have in the past. Instead of routinely presenting my list of petitions to God so that He can honor me by fulfilling them, I see prayer as a *relationship* between God and me. I come to Him to commune with Him, to love Him and be loved in return. (Of course, it's really the other way around: God first loved me, and I love Him in response! But because of this, the circle continues round and round—God loving me, me loving God, endless adoration. Therefore, I can come to Him each day, already loving Him, for love once begun need never end.)

And because God loves me, He is interested in every detail of my life. He wants me to make requests of Him, to reach out in love into the lives of my family and friends and the world to intercede in their behalf. Whereas in the past I often questioned why God did not answer all my prayers in just the way I expected Him to, I am now learning to trust Him completely, not questioning why He didn't follow all my suggestions. It's obvious to me in so many ways that my understanding of events and people is limited, whereas God can see clearly the past, present, and even the future. So why should I complain when He doesn't follow *my* recommendations? I know He has heard my requests and will take care of the situation in the best way possible.

It does not make me less vocal in prayer about conditions and people, however. You see, God has made each of us to be a part of the network of humanity, to help bear one another's burdens. Prayer, in some special way we cannot understand fully, allows God to do things He could not do if we did not pray. God is not limited in power, but He has *voluntarily* restricted Himself in order to give humanity complete free will. When I pray, it allows God His own freedom to work within His plan. So, if anything, I am *more* vocal about people and situations than in the past. But I am less rigid, less controlling, in my demands for suitable answers to my prayers. I am learning to trust in the permanence of my relationship with God rather than continually testing it by how often He answers my prayers in the way I expect Him to.

Thus my prayer expands beyond formal devotional times to encompass me day and night. It is a hand-in-hand, heart-in-heart relationship. Jesus spoke of His relationship with His Father ("the Father is in me, and I in the Father" [John 10:38]) and added His desire that His earth children join in that intimate circle: "May they also be in us so that the world may believe that you have sent me" (John 17:21).

How can I speak of this subject so positively? It's because I have discovered this glorious relationship described throughout Scripture!

When God declared that He made humanity in His own image, He gave us the first glimpse of how close He meant for the relationship between God and human beings to be. As children grow up to be in the image of their parents, so God created children for Himself.

One day when our oldest son had his first permanent job, my husband went to the office where he worked. A surprised receptionist greeted him before he even opened his mouth. "Why, you're John Shewmake's father, aren't you?" she asked.

Our son, John, Jr., had grown up to look so much like his father that the relationship was immediately visible.

That's the way God planned it to be for His earth children. Not likeness in physical looks alone, of course, but in thoughts, desires, abilities, and actions His children were to be like Him. Sin, however, changed God's original plan.

In the Garden of Eden, before the entrance of sin, He spoke face-to-face with His children, and they heard Him with their physical ears. After Adam and Eve rebelled, although they repented and God reinstated them as His children, He was no longer able to approach them face-to-face. They could no longer look upon His brightness and perfection and live. The thunder of His voice would cause them to tremble with fear for their lives. (Read the story of Sinai in Exodus 19 and 20.) So God, in His love and mercy, instituted the prayer relationship so that humanity could hear God with the inward ear and respond in human words, either thoughts or audibly spoken. It is only within this relationship that we can hear and understand the voice of God.

The Bible gives numerous illustrations of just how close God desired the relationship between His children and Himself to be. When He chose the descendants of Abraham to be His special people and led them forth from Egypt, God said, "I will walk among you and be your God, and you will be my people" (Lev. 26:12). As their God He promised to love them, protect them from their enemies, feed them, and heal their diseases. Even their shoes did not wear out during their 40-year trek in the desert! In response, He required of them, "You are to be holy to me because I, the Lord, am holy, and I have set you apart from the nations to be *my own*" (Lev. 20:26). *God desired an intimate family relationship with His people.*

He illustrated this close relationship in numerous ways so that no one could miss the meaning of what He had in mind:

God is the Father, we the children (Jer. 3:19).

God is the husband, we the wife (Jer. 3:20).

God is the shepherd, we the sheep (Eze. 34:12, 13).

All the way through the Old Testament He words and re-words His plaintive desire for this intimate family relationship with His people, one that has constant communication back and forth. It is the central theme of the entire Bible.

The covenant circle tightens as the New Testament reveals Jesus, both God and man. There we see the Father-Son relationship in action in the life of Christ. We watch Jesus awaken early each morning to talk with His Father, and observe Him listen for instructions throughout the day.

What voice did Jesus hear in His day-by-day relationship with His Father? Was it an audible one?

The Gospels tell us of three times that Jesus heard the audible voice of God: at His baptism (Matt. 3:17), on the Mount of Transfiguration (Matt. 17:5), and in the Temple just before His death (John 12:28). Note that when God spoke in audible words that last time in the Temple, Jesus said to the people, "This voice was for your benefit, not mine" (verse 30). Evidently the human Jesus found greater blessing for Himself in the inward voice of the Spirit than in God's audible voice.

It's an interesting study to search out the ways God spoke to His people in Bible times. Sometimes He communicated in audible tones. He was able to talk with Moses as with a friend and called out to Paul on the Damascus road. But more often He reached His people through dreams and thoughts. It seems that

an audible voice was normally too disconcerting and frightening to be helpful. The still small inward voice of the Holy Spirit
was more likely to be a daily guide.

David, the songwriter and singer of Israel, found great comfort in the inward voice of God. "Hear my voice when I call, O
Lord," he says in Psalm 27:7, 8; "be merciful to me and answer
me. My heart says of you, 'Seek his face!' Your face, Lord, I will
seek." In his heart David heard the call to search for the face of
God. And he responded wholeheartedly.

Jesus spoke often of the inward voice. He repeated over and
over again, "He who has ears, let him hear" (Matt. 11:15; 13:9,
43; Mark 4:23; Luke 14:35; Rev. 2:7). That He was speaking of
the inward voice and the understanding response of the heart is
clearly explained in the context of the Matthew 13 statement,
where He quotes from Isaiah 6:9, 10:

> "You will be ever hearing but never understanding;
>   you will be ever seeing but never perceiving.
> For this people's heart has become calloused;
>   they hardly hear with their ears,
>   and they have closed their eyes.
> Otherwise they might see with their eyes,
>   hear with their ears,
>   understand with their hearts
>   and turn, and I would heal them" (Matt. 13:14, 15).

In the parable of the shepherd and his flock Jesus explains
about the variety of inward voices. "I tell you the truth, the man
who does not enter the sheep pen by the gate, but climbs in by
some other way, is a thief and a robber. The man who enters by
the gate is the shepherd of his sheep. The watchman opens the
gate for him, and the sheep listen to his voice. He calls his own
sheep by name and leads them out. When he has brought out
all his own, he goes on ahead of them, and his sheep follow him
because they know his voice. But they will never follow a
stranger; in fact, they will run away from him because they do
not recognize a stranger's voice. . . . *My sheep listen to my*

voice; I know them, and they follow me" (John 10:1-27).

The people of Israel built large sheep pens conveniently located among the pasturelands so that the shepherd could protect his flocks at night from lions, wolves, bears, and other predators. Often several flocks with their shepherds would spend the night in a single pen. In the morning the shepherds separated the sheep as each herdsman called his own animals by name. They responded only to the familiar voice of their own shepherd, ignoring the others.

Learning to listen to and identify the voice of God in our daily lives is crucial to maintaining that intimate family relationship with God which will ensure a continual sense of His presence.

Summary

God chose only one avenue to commune with humanity—the human mind. The inward voice of the Holy Spirit, heard with the heart or mind, is God's way of reaching us and impressing truth upon our hearts.

But Satan can also use the mind to impress error, even to quoting Scripture as He did with Jesus.

The only safe way to identify the voice of God is to have a daily *relationship* with Him (God loving me, and I loving God in response).

God initiated this relationship in the Garden of Eden right after sin entered, as soon as Adam and Eve had responded to His call to repentance. Although they could no longer speak to God face-to-face because of sin, yet He reinstated them as His children, planting His laws within their hearts, enabling them to hear Him speak in their hearts or minds even when they did not hear His actual voice with their ears. It is within this relationship that we can hear God speak.

God gives us several illustrations in the Bible of the intimate family relationship He desires for us so that we can understand just what He has in mind:

God the Father, we the children (Jer. 3:19).

God the husband, we the wife (Jer. 3:20).

God the shepherd, we the sheep (Eze. 34:12, 13).

Jesus as human reveals just how close and intimate God desires this relationship to be. He heard the voice of God in just the same way we do.

Our Saviour explained in the story of the good shepherd (John 10) how the sheep know their shepherd's voice from the other voices: the one who enters by the gate is the shepherd. Anyone approaching them by any other way is a robber. The sheep recognize the voice of their shepherd and pay no attention to any other. The shepherd calls his sheep by name, and they follow him.

(An interesting study is to explore the Bible for references to the intimate family relationship God desires to have with us. It is often referred to as God's everlasting covenant.)

CHAPTER TWO

The Trysting Place

"Tryst—an appointment to meet at a specified time and place, especially one made secretly by lovers"—*Webster's New World Dictionary,* 2nd ed.

The best way to begin our cultivation of hearing God's voice is to plan a daily prayer time. In the last chapter we found that it is always His desire to have an intimate family relationship with every human being. He created us to be His children. Although we lost that relationship through sin, when we experience the new birth we once again become God's dearly loved children. God speaks to us today just as He did to His children in Bible times. What we need to cultivate is the atmosphere conducive to hearing His voice.

Each person differs in personality, in lifestyle, and in culture, and God approaches each of us within our limits. What I am sharing in this book is a list of ways that have proved helpful to me in hearing His voice in my daily life. Perhaps you will find some of my suggestions beneficial in your own life.

I was 19 years old when I made a total commitment to serve God and became conscious of God's desire for a personal relationship with me. Although I grew up in a Seventh-day Adventist Christian home, it was the first time I caught a glimpse of the depth of His love. Because of the daily example of my godly parents, I began to realize that I could better walk with God if I began each day with Him. In those days the Missionary Volunteer Department of the General Conference published a small Morning Watch booklet that devoted a page for each month, listing a Bible text to look up and read each morning. So I purchased a booklet for myself and followed this plan, reading the designated verse for the day and then praying briefly. Most likely I spent only five minutes in my morning devotions, yet it set the direction of my day. I thought about God during the day, wrote poetry about Him, and talked about Him with my friends. In my young romantic way He became my lover, and my morning time with Him a trysting place. Consciously belonging to God brought me a peace I had never known before.

God blessed me not only with peace, but also by guiding my life. I began dating a young ministerial student at the college I attended, and we married one week after he graduated. Then one week after our wedding we began our work in the ministry. During the early days of our service the church sent interns out to work with evangelists in series of meetings. And those evangelists kept us busy setting up tents, spreading sawdust, tending cranky oil stoves, running movie projectors, leading song services, taking up offerings, and later visiting the people who attended the meetings and giving Bible studies in their homes. We stayed up late at night and got up early in the morning, living in tiny trailers behind the tents or in small apartments. Needless to say, we moved often!

I found it hard to maintain even my simple short devotional life, for I never seemed to be alone. Oh, I read the Bible and prayed, but it all seemed to be a part of my work. Somehow my work for God seemed to have swallowed up my personal relationship with Him.

And then, after two and a half years of marriage, the children began to come. John and I had both looked forward to having a family, and we were delighted. But the children effectively put a stop to my attending so many meetings and accompanying John in visitation. We had four children in a period of four years and three months. Now, of course, I was busier than I had ever been before. By this time my husband was pastoring a church of his own, and I had my responsibilities as a pastor's wife in addition to taking care of my children.

We had no automatic washing machines, no gas driers, no permanent press materials, no disposable diapers. I felt lucky to have an electric washing machine with a wringer (a definite improvement over the way my mother had washed clothes when her children were small!), but I had to put the clothes through two rinses by hand and feed them through a wringer three times and then hang them on outdoor lines to dry in the sun. Later I figured that I washed diapers every day except Sabbath for six and a half years!

Added to that was the starching and ironing. Ministers wore a clean white shirt every day, with a change for the evening if they were attending a meeting. That meant I had at *least* seven white shirts a week to wash, starch, and iron—most likely nine or 10. Of course, the children's and my things must be ironed as well, plus pillow slips, dresser scarves, tablecloths, and whatever else was necessary for proper housekeeping. (For years I even ironed the sheets!)

All that, along with caring for four babies, cooking, dishwashing, and housecleaning—well, it even makes me tired to remember! Of course, I also led the children's divisions for Sabbath school and entertained guests for Sabbath dinner, baked pies for Dorcas bake sales, and did whatever else I was asked to do.

So what had happened to my morning times with God? Because I seldom woke up naturally, even my short devotions were out of the question. Usually an emergency jerked me awake—a baby crying or a small boy tugging at my arm. I never had enough sleep.

Yet I enjoyed both my roles—mother and pastor's wife. I think that if I hadn't married a minister, I would have chosen to be one myself. (If I'd been a man, of course! Women scarcely dreamed of the ministry for themselves in those days.)

The years when my children were small I remember as some of the happiest days of my life. I delighted in each new accomplishment of each child. If we had been financially well off, we would have had a dozen children!

It was only the lack of time that bothered me. And the terrible physical tiredness and insufficient sleep.

Then God took the initiative. He began calling me to a closer walk with Him. As I worked I sensed a yearning to read the Bible and pray, to know God's will in every part of my life, to hear His voice and worship Him. But I could find no time. Sometimes, when by chance all the babies were quiet at once, I would sit down and open my Bible to read. But the same thing happened every time—I fell asleep! Reading the children's Sabbath school lesson to them each evening, along with rushing around on Friday evening to prepare my Sabbath school program for the next day, was all the Bible study I managed to do. I never heard a sermon through. Oh, I was sitting in church, all right, but I had four children to amuse and keep quiet. Even our weekend company gave me little adult or spiritual conversation. I had meals to prepare, children to feed, and dishes to do.

I know God understood. But the amazing thing about Him is that He *always* has a way for us to maintain a relationship with Him, even when it seems humanly impossible.

One evening about 10:00, as I was standing at the ironing board doing a white shirt for my husband to wear the next day, I felt God's initiative again.

"My Father," I responded silently, "how I long to spend time with You. But it's impossible for me to have morning devotions. I never get enough sleep to wake up naturally. If I set an alarm to awaken me, I'd be too sleepy to study or pray. I'd just fall asleep, as I do in the daytime when I try to read. At any rate, if an alarm went off in this little house, I'd immediately have three little boys in bed with me! So You can see it's impossible."

I stood on one foot and then the other, trying to rest one weary leg at a time as I continued ironing.

"Father," I continued, "I figure that it'll be about 10 years before I'm able to have regular morning devotions again!" But then, led by the Holy Spirit, in desperation I added, "O my Father, I can't wait that long! Who's going to show me how to be a mother, how to teach my children, how to be a pastor's wife? *I need You now.* So I have a plan. I'm going to take my Bible with me tonight and put it on the nightstand beside my bed. Then I'm asking You to awaken me at least a half hour before my little early birds awaken. And wake me up with a clear mind so that I can commune with You. If You do this in the morning, I will know that You have heard my prayer and answered me."

With eager expectation I told my husband what I had petitioned God to do and asked if it would bother him too much if I turned on the light by my side of the bed when I awoke in the morning. (There was just no way that I could risk getting out of bed and going anywhere else in the house. The boys heard the slightest sound that near to their rising time.) My husband assured me the light wouldn't bother him. He'd just put the pillow over his head. So, laying my Bible on the nightstand, I went to bed.

God responded to my prayer! Every morning, day after day, week after week, and year after year, He awakened me with a clear mind ready to study and pray before the children woke up. Of course, in a few years I was able to move to the living room for my prayer time. But this constant daily miracle changed my life and thrilled my soul. It gave me new life in child care, in housework, and in church work.

Several years later, to my delight, I discovered a verse in the Bible in which God promises to awaken all His children just as He did me!

> "The Sovereign Lord has given me an instructed tongue,
>   to know the word that sustains the weary.
> *He wakens me morning by morning,*
>   *wakens my ear to listen like one being taught"*
> (Isa. 50:4).

It is, of course, a prophecy of what God the Father was going to do for God the Son when He came as a human being, to maintain that intimate family relationship with Him. But whatever God did for Jesus He promises to do for us. So the verse is a promise for every child of God. It shows us how we can respond and cooperate with Him in His initiative to maintain a relationship with us.

Although it is God's initiative, our response determines whether it will work. I could have chosen to go back to sleep after He awakened me. God always leaves us free. But I *loved* that time with Him, and I was so excited about His awakening me that I never even thought about going back to sleep. Thus began a lifelong habit of rising early to talk with God before the day began.

The early-morning hours are the best time to commune with God for a number of reasons. The night's rest has slowed down our bodies and minds. The house around us is quiet, the telephone is not ringing. Even the outdoors surrounding us is still. Traffic is slow. The world is preparing for dawn, and the day sounds of animal life have not yet begun. The birds are just beginning their morning chorus. We have not yet tackled the day's work and so will not be so easily distracted. In quietness we can more clearly discern the voice of God.

> "In the morning, O Lord, you hear my voice;
> in the morning I lay my requests before you
> and wait in expectation" (Ps. 5:3).

> "Because of the Lord's great love we
> are not consumed,
> for his compassions never fail.
> They are new every morning;
> great is your faithfulness" (Lam. 3:22, 23).

> "Morning by morning he dispenses his justice,
> and every new day he does not fail" (Zeph. 3:5).

Even after a busy day of healing people, Jesus arose before it was light and sought a solitary place to pray (Mark 1:35).

For the majority of people, morning is the best time to begin cultivating hearing the voice of God. Work, lifestyle, and personality may produce exceptions. However, whenever your day begins, that is the time to renew your life with God and to pledge to serve Him that day. Your first decisions and choices of the day set its tenor. And I assure you that whatever your circumstances, however busy you are, whatever the lifestyle of those around you, God will work with you to discover the best time for you to commune meaningfully with Him. He has a way to set *your* life in order so that you will have ample time to spend with Him.

Several years ago I discovered a helpful quotation from Ellen White on this subject. I was an academy librarian at the time, and one morning just before classes began, one of the sixth-grade teachers hurried in, searched through the shelf of Ellen White books, and picked up a volume. He turned quickly toward the checkout desk as he shuffled through its pages. As he approached the desk he apparently found what he was looking for and exclaimed in an exultant voice, "It's still there! It's still there on page 90!"

His excitement amused me. As I checked out the copy of *Messages to Young People* to him, I asked what it was that he was so pleased to still find on page 90.

"Read page 90," he admonished me as he hurried off to class just as the bell began to ring.

As soon as I could, I found a copy of *Messages to Young People* and turned to page 90. Here is what I read:

"When you rise in the morning, do you feel your helplessness, and your need of strength from God? and do you humbly, heartily make known your wants to your heavenly Father? If so, angels mark your prayers, and if these prayers have not gone forth out of feigned lips, when you are in danger of unconsciously doing wrong, and exerting an influence which will lead others to do wrong, your guardian angel will be by your side, prompting you to a better course, choosing your words for you, and influencing your actions.

"If you feel in no danger, and if you offer no prayer for help and strength to resist temptations, you will be sure to go astray; your neglect of duty will be marked in the book of God in heaven, and you will be found wanting in the trying day."

No wonder the sixth-grade teacher was excited! If only we could catch a glimpse of what God longs to do for us continually.

As soon as I began a relationship with Jesus I discovered that in order to hear His voice clearly in my heart, I needed to find a trysting place where God and I could converse alone. I believe that will be your experience, too. Listening to God's voice in the quietness will prepare you to recognize His voice in the tumult of life as the day progresses.

Summary

The best place to begin cultivating the voice of God is by purposefully planning a daily prayer period. The atmosphere of a morning quiet time with God is especially conducive to hearing Him speak.

God takes the initiative in this and promises to awaken each of us to listen to His voice (Isa. 50:4).

Although He takes the first step, yet our response determines whether it will work. It is our decision to arise and pray. If we ignore God's voice, we will soon no longer hear it.

The morning hours are a good time to talk with God because:

1. Our bodies and minds have slowed down.
2. The house around us is quiet.
3. Life outdoors is calm. Even nature is tranquil.
4. We have not yet started our day's work and so are not as easily distracted.
5. We have the example of Jesus.
6. Prayer sets the tone for our day.

Learning to hear God's voice in the quietness prepares us to recognize His voice in the daily tumult of life.

CHAPTER THREE

What Shall I Talk About?

*W*hen God began awakening me every morning to pray and study, it really excited me, because I felt sure that soon I would be perfect! You will recall that when I began a morning time with God as a girl my devotions consisted of one Bible verse and a short prayer. Now, as my family responsibilities increased and as my thinking matured, I realized that I needed more time with God than that, so I always allowed at least half an hour for my devotions. As time went by it dawned on me that I was still far from perfect. In fact, it looked unlikely that I would ever be!

Then God again took the initiative. He led me at last to realize that my only hope was in *constant communion* with Him throughout the day. I could not rely just on a morning prayer alone. Soon I began to see that true prayer is not just a measured segment of time, but a walk with God just as Enoch had. God talks, I answer, and God speaks again, my every thought and action under His control. Of course, that doesn't happen immediately. But it is a goal that I am working toward.

So far I have made two suggestions on how to cultivate hearing the divine voice. The first one is to realize that the only way to communicate with God is within an intimate family *relationship* with Him. The new birth is the doorway to such a relationship. Second, we should set aside a regular morning time to spend with Him—a trysting place for just the two of us. God created us as intelligent beings, and although He takes the initiative in calling us to Himself, yet He leaves it to each of us to choose whether to respond. He will never decide for us. Unless we answer the yearning He plants within us by deliberately—and maybe even painfully—arising earlier to spend time with Him, it will never happen.

But daily devotions are not magic. I didn't automatically become perfect after years of waking up early to pray. Each of us always has one step more to take. When I began to realize that even my half hour study and prayer times were inadequate for the growth I needed, I asked God to show me what I should do next. I tried a longer prayer time, timing myself by the clock, as one intense young man had suggested to me. But I didn't have enough to talk about for an hour with God. Imagine that! I, a talkative extrovert, couldn't fill up a whole hour with the Lord. Right then I knew I needed help badly.

God began to open up to me the secrets of His plan of redemption as revealed through the sanctuary. I saw that the sanctuary, as God had directed Moses to set it up in the wilderness, did more than show me the future of God's people and the world—it also revealed to me what He was presently doing in my life. The steps the priests took daily in the sanctuary service demonstrated how God is working to save *me* from sin. When I sought to cooperate with Him in the work He was doing in my life, I suddenly found that I had plenty to talk about! In fact, an hour could not cover it, for God had undertaken a 24-hour-a-day program in me. So I must be ready to listen and hear His voice and speak to Him day *and* night.

Because I have described sanctuary prayer in detail in my books on prayer, I will list here only the daily steps to personal prayer that the sanctuary reveals:

Praise as we enter His courts.

Repentance and confession at the altar of sacrifice.

Daily cleansing, emptying of self and sin, and rebaptism at the laver.

Daily infilling of the Holy Spirit at the lampstand.

Spiritual food for growth, obedience, and action at the table of shewbread.

Intercessory prayer for others at the altar of incense.

Meeting the judgment that involves investigation, discipline, and instruction in the Most Holy Place.

Following the sanctuary steps in my morning prayer time gives me *focus, order, progression,* and *completeness.* It reveals to me a more complete picture of God. I *focus* on specifics: specific sins, specific forgiveness, the reality of cleansing, Spirit infilling, and growth. It provides *order* to my thoughts. I see how God is working. The steps of sanctuary prayer move me along so that I don't get bogged down in self-pity or even obsessive self-examination (as important as that is to recognizing truth), but bring *progress* to encompass the entire picture God has in mind for me. When I have completed my prayer I sense the reality of God's *complete* sacrifice, His *complete* cleansing and redemption. I can place my hand in His and walk on through my day, confident that I will hear His voice.

Because the practice of sanctuary prayer has been such a personal blessing to me, I urge all of you to try it. Yet I know that God is not arbitrary. Not everyone has to pray this way. Many great Christians have never heard of sanctuary prayer. However, I suspect that their prayers follow many of the same steps the sanctuary reveals. Or perhaps the understanding of sanctuary prayer is one of God's special gifts to His last-day people, showing us a way to quickly catch hold of what He is constantly doing for us in the judgment. At least it has been one of His special gifts to *me.*

Thus, my third suggestion for learning to listen to the voice of God is to follow the progression the sanctuary reveals for knowing God and understanding ourselves. In order to do this, you may want to reread the story of how He led the descendants of Abraham out of Egypt to be His special people, reviewing especially the layout and furniture of the wilderness sanctuary, including the sacrifices (Exodus, Leviticus, Numbers, and Deuteronomy). Also, my book *Sanctuary Secrets to Personal Prayer* will give you ideas for using the sanctuary steps in your personal prayer. Another helpful book on the sanctuary is *The Cross and Its Shadow,* by Stephen Haskell (published originally in 1914, but reprinted in 1970 by Southern Publishing Association and still available in a paperback facsimile reproduction). Stephen Haskell says in his preface:

"There is no other subject which so fully unites all parts of the inspired Word into one harmonious whole as the subject of the sanctuary. Every gospel truth centers in the sanctuary service, and radiates from it like the rays from the sun.

"Every type used in the entire sacrificial system was designed by God to bear resemblance to some spiritual truth. The value of these types consisted in the fact that they were chosen by God Himself to shadow forth the different phases of the complete plan of redemption, made possible by the death of Christ. The likeness between type and antitype is never accidental, but is simply a fulfillment of the great plan of God."

One afternoon during the break in a two-hour seminar on sanctuary prayer that I was conducting, a woman told me a story that especially touched my heart. She had attended a women's retreat a few months before, and at one of the services the leader invited those present to share how the Lord was working personally in their lives. This woman related to me the story of Mary, one of the young women at the retreat.

Mary had been hospitalized for a life-threatening illness. Diligent in prayer, she also knew that she had good doctors, so she felt certain that the outcome would be positive. However, one afternoon several doctors filed into her hospital room and solemnly told her that they had done all that they knew medically to do, but her body was not responding. She would just have to prepare to die. Stunned, Mary was silent. After the doctors left she spoke to God.

"Lord," Mary said, "I felt certain that You meant for me to live. I'm young and have so much to live for. I'm just starting out in my lifework. But if it is Your will that I should die, I'm willing to die. I have just one request. During the days, weeks, or months that I have yet to live I want to know You in as close a way as it is possible for a human being to know God. That is my one request."

They sent Mary home from the hospital soon after that. One

day she heard about sanctuary prayer and felt impressed that it was the way to know God that she had requested. So she began the daily practice of sanctuary prayer. Within a few weeks she realized that she was getting well. At the time Mary told her story at the retreat she was back at work and in good health.

"Sanctuary prayer is my health," she said.

Although Mary received physical healing, yet I believe the real theme of the story was not healing, but *acceptance and submission.* No longer asking for physical healing, she had submitted completely to God and accepted whatever was His will.

That young woman's story so touched me that nearly every day I pray her prayer.

"Dear Lord, help me to know You today in as close a way as it is possible for a human being to know God."

Following the sanctuary steps for daily prayer gives us the assurance that we are talking to God about the vital issues of salvation and opens up our ears to hear God as He communes with us.

Summary

Although God calls us to begin the day with Him, daily devotions in and of themselves are not magical. Just the fact that we pray every morning offers no guarantee that we will grow as we should. God is summoning us to a constant walk with Him, as did Enoch: us talking, God talking—a continual relationship.

He has given us an illustration of how He is working in our lives through the model of the sanctuary described in Exodus and Leviticus. By following the steps that the priests took in their service in our morning prayers, we can understand what God wants to do in our lives. Studying into the meaning of these services helps us to intelligently cooperate with Him in the work He is doing for us.

The sanctuary reveals the following steps:

Praise as we enter His courts.

Repentance and confession at the altar of sacrifice.

Daily cleansing, emptying of self and sin, and rebaptism at the laver.

Daily infilling of the Holy Spirit at the lampstand.

Spiritual food for growth, obedience, and action at the table of shewbread.

Intercessory prayer for others at the altar of incense.

Meeting the judgment that involves investigation, discipline, and instruction in the Most Holy Place.

Employing the sanctuary steps for daily prayer gives us the assurance that we are talking to God about the vital issues of salvation and opens up our ears to hear God as He communes with us.

CHAPTER FOUR

Words in Our Own Language

I have suggested three ways to help cultivate our hearing of the voice of God: one, recognizing that God created us to be His family and that He desires an intimate family relationship with us; two, setting aside a special time every day alone with God; three, following the sanctuary steps that He uses for turning sinners into saints. These three ways of learning to listen are the foundation for opening our spiritual ears to hear.

The fourth way to cultivate listening is just as important. *Accept the words of Scripture as God's voice to us personally.*

I have heard people say when introduced to some Bible teaching they are reluctant to adopt, "Well, when God tells me that personally, I'll believe it."

In reality every word in the Bible has a personal message for us. The function of the inward voice of the Holy Spirit is to help us understand the written word or to address a specific problem or circumstance of our lives, not to take the place of the necessity of studying the Bible. And even then the Holy Spirit often uses the words of Scripture as He speaks to us.

To put it another way, God is not going to come to me and say, "Carrol, I don't want you to steal." He has already told me that in His Word. But I may hear the voice of the Holy Spirit dealing with me specifically, explaining to me that when I am habitually late to appointments I am robbing the time of other people. Or when I gossip He may tell me that I am stealing the reputation of another.

When I use the title "Words in Our Own Language," I do not have in mind English, Portuguese, Italian, or some other modern tongue, necessary as it is that we each have the Bible in the language we speak. Rather I mean the language of the *heart*. The Holy Spirit takes the words of the Bible and applies them to my specific circumstances and needs. The world has such an impact on us that it is often hard to think spiritually. The apostle Paul puts it this way: "The man without the Spirit does not accept the things that come from the Spirit of God, for they are foolishness to him, and he *cannot understand them,* because they are spiritually discerned" (1 Cor. 2:14).

God expects us to cultivate spiritual discernment. For a long time I wondered why God kept telling us to search for Him when in the Bible stories it was obvious that God Himself does the searching. He always takes the initiative in our relationship. God called out to Adam and Eve as they hid in the garden, "Where are you?" He does the same for us. But not too long ago it came to me that *seeking* God is our response to His initiative. Instead of just sitting back and basking in His smile when He finds us, He expects us to put our all into the relationship, just as He has. We are to turn and hunt for Him with our whole heart. The Holy Spirit, speaking through the prophet Jeremiah, said: "You will seek me and find me when you seek me with all your heart" (Jer. 29:13).

Even in His initial encounter with us God values our individuality and free will. He seeks us, then waits for us to turn and search for Him. Our seeking is vital to the relationship. Jesus tells us what will happen when we have developed that two-way relationship with God: "Ask and it will be given to you; seek and you will find; knock and the door will be opened to you. For everyone who asks receives; he who seeks finds; and to him who knocks, the door will be opened" (Matt. 7:7, 8).

The best way that I have found to cultivate spiritual discernment is to spend time seeking God through reading Scripture. This is not merely reading as you would a story. It is continually asking yourself, What is God saying in this passage to my heart? Eventually our minds will become open to God's thoughts as a flower responds to the sun and rain. The Bible will become intensely interesting to us, for it will be like a personal letter from a father or lover. And God will be able to take great delight in the intimacy of our relationship.

I find that God speaks to me through Scripture in two different ways. Sometimes as I am reading—or someone else is reading—the Bible, certain passages will be illumined in my mind. If I am reading for myself, it will almost seem as though a marker has highlighted them. In fact, I have sometimes checked back to see if they were! If someone else is reading the passage aloud, it may almost seem as though I hear God's actual voice.

The second way God uses Scripture to speak to me is to bring words that I have read in the past to my remembrance at a time when I am not actually reading the Bible. This inward voice of God speaks with authority and power, and creates in me the same sense of joy as when I find God speaking to me as I read. In either way God may be admonishing me, teaching me, or comforting me. I find joy even in His discipline. In fact, that is one of the ways we can tell God's voice from that of Satan. Satan has employed Scripture to deceive (Matt. 4:6). But an important difference exists between God's voice and Satan's. When Satan reminds us of our sins, he taunts us with them, and we become discouraged and miserable. But when God shows us our sins He offers hope and pardon, and brings us a sense of joy in His presence.

One time in our lives my husband and I discovered that we had made a grave error in judgment in financial matters. It looked as though we might have to face serious consequences. Life looked dark indeed. We had lost our sense of God's presence. In fact, I wondered if He wasn't just plain disgusted with us!

One afternoon I knelt by the bed praying. "O Lord," I cried, "are we going to lose it all—our reputations, our jobs, and everything we own? What are Your plans for us? Are You just going to let us crash?" The darkness around me was as deep as if it had been midnight.

It had been a long time since I had been conscious of the inward voice of God in my heart. Pain and desperation had so filled me that I was unable to hear anything else. But now God spoke. "I know the plans I have for you," He said.

Immediately I recognized the inward voice of God. And I felt certain that His words were part of a Scripture verse. Still on my knees, I reached out for my Bible. Yes, there the verse was: "'For I know the plans I have for you,' declares the Lord, 'plans to prosper you and not to harm you, plans to give you hope and a future'" (Jer. 29:11).

This time He had quoted only part of the wonderful promise, leaving it to me to read for myself from the Bible the beautiful future He had in store for me. The pain vanished, although my circumstances remained exactly the same. It took years to rectify the error in judgment, but we walked that road in the light of God's presence.

Another time I was deep in the heartache of a breakup in a relationship with someone I dearly loved. I could see it coming but could find no way to avert it. One day the person lent me a special book, one irreplaceable if lost, for the title page contained a personal inscription from the author. Because of this, I hesitated to borrow the book. What if something happened to it? I wanted nothing to hasten the end of our relationship. But I did want to read the book. I would read it quickly, I decided, and return it within a day or two. That would be safe.

Although I did read the book immediately, I also got busy, and before I knew it several weeks had gone by. Then one afternoon I suddenly remembered that I had not yet returned the volume. Immediately I went to the place I remembered putting it, planning to take it back that very afternoon.

The book was not there. I began searching the house, confident I'd find it soon. Because we have many books, looking for a specific one in our house is like hunting for a needle in a haystack. After I had checked all the places that I could think of where I might have casually laid down a book, I began examining the bookshelves book by book. Two double floor-to-ceiling bookshelves in the living room, two of the same in the study, two single floor-to-ceiling bookshelves in the bedroom—each shelf book by book. By now I was in panic. I had been praying as I searched, but finally decided that perhaps I should kneel and pray in a way that God couldn't possibly ignore!

Dropping to the floor by the bed, I began to pour out my heart to Him.

"O Lord," I prayed aloud, "I've got to find that book. Where is it? I can't have lost it. I'll never be forgiven if I have. Oh, *where* is that book?" Panic took over.

"O Father, what kind of person am I that I would lose something that means so much to someone else? I'm just a horrible and untrustworthy person. No one would want me for a friend. I'm absolutely hopeless."

By that time tears washed away any words that I could speak, but it was not silent in the room. Loud crying filled the house. I'm not usually a crying person, and seldom weep. Yet the crying continued on and on. Finally, realizing that I was in no condition to continue praying, I arose from my knees.

Glancing through my tears at the clock, I suddenly realized that I was due at a meeting in a little more than an hour. It was time for me to get ready. Perhaps the water in the shower would shock me enough to quiet my crying. But it didn't work. In fact, my sobs seemed to increase rather than diminish. About that time I noticed that the window in the bathroom was open, and I began to fear that the neighbors would hear me and come to investigate. In desperation, I stuffed the washcloth in my mouth and stifled the sobs.

Later, clothed in my robe, I sat in the rocking chair beside my bed and tried to compose myself before I dressed. My husband hurried in to prepare for an appointment of his own. Looking at me closely, he asked how I was.

"Oh, fine," I replied. "I'm just getting ready to go to my meeting."

"You look like you've been crying," he commented.

I made no reply, because I felt certain that if I began to explain I would start all over again. We were both in a hurry, so neither of us mentioned my tears again.

On the way to the church I wondered how I was going to get

anything out of the service in my state of mind. Yet the speaker was a special friend, and I wanted to support her.

I really have no remembrance of what the topic was for the evening. My only memory is of one Bible verse the speaker read: "During the days of Jesus' life on earth, he offered up prayers and petitions with *loud cries and tears* to the one who could save him from death, and he was heard because of his reverent submission" (Heb. 5:7).

Loud cries and tears! "O Jesus," I inwardly exclaimed, "do You mean that You felt like I did this afternoon? You know how I feel?" The sense of God's presence swept over me as I realized that He had been with me all that long afternoon, weeping along with me at my panic and self-hatred. The load lifted from my shoulders as I shifted it to Him.

As I entered my bedroom to prepare for bed after the meeting, the phone rang. Sinking down into the chair beside the phone, I answered it. As I talked I absentmindedly lifted up a magazine on the table by the phone and discovered the book I had been searching for all afternoon.

"Forgive me, Lord," I prayed as I once more knelt beside my bed. "Forgive me for my panic and lack of faith. Oh, I know You are always beside me. But thank You so much for speaking to me through Your Word. What a comfort it is to know that You are personally acquainted with loud cries and tears. That verse will always have special meaning for me."

Half the battle is won when we begin to consistently remember that the words of Scripture are God's words to us personally, spoken *in the language of our own individual hearts.*

Summary

In the first three chapters of this book I have suggested three ways to help cultivate hearing God's voice:

1. Recognize that God created us to be His family and that He desires to have an intimate family relationship with us.

2. Set aside a special time every morning to be alone with Him.

3. Follow the steps the sanctuary shows us for turning sin-

ners into saints.

The fourth step is *to accept the words of Scripture as God's voice to us personally.* When God tells us in His Word not to lie or steal, we do not need to expect that He will individually, by His inward voice, repeat this to us. He has already told us this clearly in His Word. However, His inward voice will *magnify* the concepts to fit our individual situation. The Holy Spirit takes the words God has spoken in the Bible and applies them to our specific circumstances and needs.

We need to *cultivate* spiritual discernment. Although God takes the initiative in seeking us, He asks us to respond by turning to and seeking Him with our whole heart. Our search for Him is vital because it takes two to have a relationship.

God speaks to me in two different ways through Scripture:

1. As I am reading (or someone else is reading aloud) I sense that the words are God's actual voice to me. It is as though a fluorescent marker has highlighted the passage.

2. At just the time I need it God brings to my memory words that I have read in the past. The words now come with power and conviction so that I readily recognize them as God's personal voice.

The words of Scripture are God's words to us personally, spoken *in the language of our own individual hearts.*

CHAPTER FIVE

Hidden in Our Hearts

The boy was failing eighth grade. The high expectations of his parents and the encouragement of his teacher seemed to do no good. He was just a dummy, he decided, just as his classmates said he was. Then the boy discovered Jesus and determined that he would not be a "dummy" in the Christian life. Each day he set aside an hour to memorize the Scriptures. Because he loved music, he often sang the verses to tunes of his own making.

Imperceptibly at first, but steadily, the boy began to do better in school. By the end of high school he was an honor student bound for college, still spending an hour a day in Bible memorization. He would grow up to be a nationally known Bible student and teacher, thrilling thousands with his Bible answers to life's dilemmas.

The man's personal testimony of what memorization of Scripture had done for him inspired my husband and me. We looked at each other as the seminar ended. Could we do it? Let's try it! we decided. Eagerly we made plans. Whole chapters—well, that sounded impossible. But we were willing to give it our best.

John and I were not children when we began our program. In fact, we were well into middle age, and we discovered that it was hard work to memorize. But we continued steadily on. I had visions of sitting around the campfire on our annual backpacking trip and reciting a complete chapter from Scripture as the firelight flickered. That would be impressive with the starry sky above and the shadowy trees our only walls.

The first scripture I memorized was Psalm 139 from *The Living Bible.* I had it well memorized before we left on our backpacking trip into the High Sierras. However, I was a little dubious about trying to quote it around the campfire. Although I knew all the words, they still came haltingly from my lips even when I was alone. With others around, it would be even more difficult.

The trail we took on that backpacking trip began with a sharp rise from a wandering creek up a dry stony mountainside strewn with huge boulders and crisscrossed with switchbacks. At best I am a slow hiker. On this trip I was worse than slow. I had foolishly purchased new boots just before leaving on the trip and found that as I trudged up that mountainside they rubbed in all the wrong places. Because I was slow, the rest of the hikers pulled far ahead. I couldn't sit down to pull off my boots and apply moleskin to my blistered feet, as I carried a heavy pack and knew that if I sat down with it on, I wouldn't be able to get up again. If I slipped out of the pack, I would be unable to put it back on unaided. So I trudged on with self-pity as my only companion. Added to the pain in my feet was my fear of heights. I always dreaded the first day out on a trail, for it was almost always the steepest. Even when I stopped to rest by leaning my pack against a tall rock, I dared not look back over the way I had come for fear of becoming dizzy and falling. Every time I had to pull up over a high rock step in the path I was sure I would lose my footing and tumble down the rocky mountainside to the bottom.

But this time God had the perfect tool to jar me out of my self-pity. Had I not hidden His words in my heart?

The words I had memorized began to run through my mind: "O Lord, you have examined my heart and know everything about me. You know when I sit or stand. When far away you know my every thought. You chart the path ahead of me, and tell me where to stop and rest. Every moment, you know where I am. You know what I am going to say before I even say it. You both precede and follow me, and place your hand of blessing on my head" (Ps. 139:1-5, TLB).

Was I alone on the rocky trail? Of course not. God was charting the path before me, choosing the rocks for me to stop at and lean upon for rest. Need I fear falling down the mountain? Why, how could I fall when God was before and behind me, and rested His hand upon my head? Suddenly I forgot the steep path and my bruised and blistered feet. I was in the temple of the Most High. As I hiked on with my unseen Companion, I quoted: "This is too glorious, too wonderful to believe! I can *never* be lost to your Spirit! I can *never* get away from my God!" (verses 6, 7, TLB).

When I caught up with the rest of my group, waiting for me in a meadow, I was almost sorry. Well, true, I was able to remove my pack and tend to my blistered feet. That was good. But the walk that morning alone with God had been beautiful beyond compare.

I had discovered that if I have hidden in my heart the words of God, they can brighten and lighten any path. Also, I realized something else. The value in memorization of Scripture does not come in public recitation but in heart-filling. I never became able to quote long portions of Scripture in public. My words always came haltingly. But the personal value was priceless.

Both my husband and I continue to memorize whole chapters or passages to fill our minds with God's thoughts. For both of us the memorizing goes slowly, perhaps because we are no longer young. Yet we are blessed both while we are memorizing and later when we recount the verses for our encouragement. And often God brings the words back into our minds at just the time we need them. Yes, it's true that we tend to forget much of what we have memorized within a few weeks, yet I doubt it ever really leaves us. Often I go back and review psalms such as 91, 51, 1, and 139, to keep them fresh in my memory.

When do we memorize? My husband does a lot of memorizing while traveling in the car. I have discovered that I memorize more quickly while walking. The physical exercise of walking seems to stimulate my mind to remember the words.

For several years, as I strolled city sidewalks, I kept a small New Testament with Proverbs and Psalms tucked into my jacket pocket for easy reference on my morning walk. Now that we have moved to the mountains, I'm looking again for the right time to memorize. John and I often circle a nearby lake for our morning walk, but instead of memorizing Scripture we are learning from God's great second book, nature.

In the past I have memorized as a part of my morning prayer-time, with a short review just before I go to bed. Also I have memorized while I ironed or cleaned house. I suspect that one could memorize while weeding or gardening or other yard work. The only ingredients necessary are a willing heart, a small Bible or portions of Scripture written on a card or piece of paper, and prayer. God is delighted to help us store His words in our hearts.

God has many ways to summon us back from our preoccupation with the world to once again behold Him. But His calling us does not eliminate our need to cooperate with Him in order to recognize His voice. That is why I am sharing the ways I have discovered to help me hear it. First, I suggested that we recognize that we are a part of God's family and that He yearns to talk with us; second, to set aside a special time each morning to meet with Him alone; third, to enlarge our concepts of what God has done and is doing in our salvation by following the steps shown us in the sanctuary; and fourth, to accept the words of Scripture as God's voice to us personally. In this chapter and the following one I'll present ways that God has shown me to familiarize myself with His words in the Bible. The better acquainted we become with Scripture, the better able we will be to hear His voice and to know for certain that it is His voice and not that of another.

In my Bible classes in grade school, academy, and college I learned proof texts and doctrines, but I never seemed to become intimately acquainted with Jesus. Unless we see the Bible as God's words to us personally, we can never have a sense of His presence. As we learn to know Him as a Father, Lover, and Friend, only then can we properly understand doctrines. Also, we will be so well acquainted with the Bible that we will be able to find the proof texts that we need. Proof texts as such never *prove* anything. The love of Jesus overflowing from one who daily walks and talks with Him demonstrates and confirms much more.

The better I came to know the Bible, the more excited I became about it. I can remember so well memorizing the entire chapter of Isaiah 40. It took me a long time, as I worked on it in the morning as part of my devotional time and reviewed at night just before I went to sleep. Although I cannot recite that chapter word for word today, yet I know what it contains. One day not long after I had memorized Isaiah 40 I read the first chapter of the book of James. When I ran across the phrase about the flower withering and dying, it produced a thrill of recognition. It echoed Isaiah 40! Again I found a similar allusion to Isaiah 40 in the first chapter of 1 Peter. At that time I was not reading from a Bible with a center reference and so Bible translators did not make such discoveries for me, but rather they were my own. More and more as I memorized I discovered the links between the different Bible writers. The Bible became intensely interesting to me.

I haven't always been a Bible student. Early in my marriage, although I loved the Lord and spent special time with Him each morning, I relaxed with storybooks. My husband never commented on it, since he knew I loved the Lord. I was faithful in studying my Sabbath school lesson, teaching, leading, and even giving Bible studies. But one evening—I remember it so clearly yet—my husband remarked to me as I was engrossed in a storybook, "What a shame it is that you don't put your good mind into something more stimulating than stories." If he had spoken it critically, self would most likely have risen up in me in rebellion. But his tone and his voice were gentle and loving. As I looked up from the page I was reading, my mouth fell open. I never forgot the regret in his words and voice. Those words began to change my reading habits. But first I had to learn to enjoy reading the Bible, to love the Word of God. That came gradually and in answer to prayer. Memorizing whole passages of Scripture played a large part in creating my interest in Bible study.

God's miracles are not like Satan's magic. He does not want to control us by any other power than love, so He draws us by His love while leaving us *free.* Thus we do not just suddenly—presto—in answer to a spoken prayer love reading the Bible. It comes in God's answer to that prayer, yes, but also by our own choice to involve ourselves with His Word. Memorization of Scripture entwines our hearts with the words of God and creates in us deep love for Him. Reading the words of Scripture with the whole heart will *always* bring us a sense of His presence.

God is still not finished with the words of Isaiah 40 in my life. The last few verses I review often to reinspire hope and courage in my heart:

"He gives strength to the weary
   and increases the power of the weak.
Even youths grow tired and weary,
   and young men stumble and fall;
but those who hope in the Lord
   will renew their strength.
They will soar on wings like eagles;
   they will run and not grow weary,
   they will walk and not be faint" (Isa. 40:29-31).

Each day this promise becomes more and more precious to me.

One morning as I was talking with God about the cleansing work He is doing in my life, I spoke regretfully of the squandered years of my life and the habit patterns that I had set during those years. I recognized that many of the problems that I daily battled in my Christian walk were cultivated tendencies that I had entrenched in my mind through years of practice. I had built up barriers and dug trenches that tended to trip me up. My situation looked hopeless to me.

But then God spoke to me from Isaiah 40:

"A voice of one calling:
'In the desert prepare
the way for the Lord;
make straight in the wilderness
a highway for our God.
Every valley shall be raised up,
every mountain and hill made low;
the rough ground shall become level,
the rugged places a plain.
And the glory of the Lord will be revealed,
and all mankind together will see it.
For the mouth of the Lord has spoken'" (verses 3-5).

"As you serve Me I will fill in the trenches or valleys that you have dug," God seemed to be saying to me, "and the mountain barriers will fall down. This is part of the work that I am doing at the laver in the sanctuary. It will happen in time if you are faithful. Thus My glory will be revealed through your life. This is My promise."

Nearly every morning in my sanctuary prayer as I come to the laver I remind God of His work that He is doing in my life. "Don't let me fail in my part," I plead. "Make me faithful and diligent."

Isaiah 40 is the prophecy of the role of John the Baptist as he announced the coming ministry of Jesus. It is also the work of the last generation of people to live on earth as they prepare the way for the second coming of Jesus and the end of sin.

"So closely," says Ellen White, "will the counterfeit resemble the true that it will be impossible to distinguish between them except by the Holy Scriptures. . . . None but those who have fortified the mind with the truths of the Bible will stand through the last great conflict" (*The Great Controversy,* pp. 593, 594).

What better way is there to hide God's truth in our hearts than through memorization of key scriptures?

Summary

David said to the Lord:

"I have hidden your word in my heart
    that I might not sin against you" (Ps. 119:11).

Memorization of Scripture is a good way to cultivate our ability to hear the inward voice of God.

The value in memorization is not in public recitation but in heart-filling.

Even though we may memorize slowly and forget quickly, yet we are blessed as we memorize and then later as we recall the verses. Often God will bring the words back into our minds at just the time we need them. While we may forget the exact words, the concepts never leave our hearts.

Suggestions for memorization:

1. Either copy the portion you want to memorize on a card or paper or carry a small New Testament with Psalms and Proverbs or a small Bible with you.

2. Memorize as you walk or drive, do housework, or work in the yard. You may memorize as a part of your morning devotional time with a short review just before you go to bed.

The better acquainted we become with Scripture, the better able we will be to hear His voice and know for certain that it is His voice and not our own thoughts or the voice of another.

Memorizing whole passages of Scripture plays a large part in creating interest for me in Bible study. It entwines my heart with the words of God and creates in me a love for God and a sense of His presence.

Ellen White tells us that the counterfeit and the true will so closely resemble each other in the end of time that only those who have filled their minds with Scripture will be able to stand (The Great Controversy, pp. 593, 594).

What better way to hide God's words in our hearts than through memorization of key scriptures?

CHAPTER SIX

Making God's Word Real

A sense of the presence of God in our daily life has a direct relationship to our faith. Believing that God is involved in my life moment by moment gives me an awareness of His presence. The apostle Paul tells us that faith comes from hearing—or reading, of course—the words of Christ (Rom. 10:17). So the more involved we become in Scripture, the greater will be our realization of His nearness and thus our ability to hear His voice.

My problem has often been how to maintain an interest in Bible reading so that it is real to me. Although I asked God to help me love to read the Bible, yet my progress seemed slow. Then I realized that God was doing His part but I also had a role to play. One of God's wonderful attributes is His recognition and appreciation of our humanity. God created us as human beings in order to have fellowship with us. He gave us the ability to choose, to think, to exercise our wills. I realized that my choice to make Scripture a very real part of my life was the missing ingredient in my learning to enjoy the Bible. When I began memorizing Scripture God created in me a love for His Word.

Since that time He has shown me other ways I can become active in Bible reading. By comparing text with text I gain new understanding of the chosen topic.

One of the most exciting concepts I have recently discovered is that *all* Bible reading can be active. We do not read the Bible in the same way as any other book. It is a message straight from heaven, not just a story to entertain us, or a book of science to comprehend by the intellect alone. The Bible is *alive.* By His Word God made the heavens and the earth, and His Word is just as creative today. We need to match the life in the Word of God with action on our part, meeting it with full heart response.

To make Bible reading active, I must realize that a passage has to do with *me.* Instead of seeing Scripture as something that happened long ago, I put myself into the stories. A. W. Tozer says that we should approach the "Bible with the idea that it is not only a book which was once spoken, but a book which is *now speaking. . . .* We may use the past tense properly to indicate that at a certain time a certain word of God was spoken, but a word of God once spoken continues to be spoken, as a child once born continues to be alive" (A. W. Tozer, *The Pursuit of God* [Harrisburg, Pa.: Christian Publications, Inc., 1948], p. 82).

Ellen White observes that "the relations between God and each soul are as distinct and full as though there were not another soul . . . for whom He gave His beloved Son" *(Steps to Christ,* p. 100).

Recognition that the whole Bible has me in mind and continually seeks to speak to me changes how I think about not only the stories but the prophecies and other passages. A. W. Tozer also comments that we should see that everything God has ever done was for each of us:

"Then we can sing: For me Thou didst cover Thyself with light as with a garment and stretch out the heavens like a curtain and lay the foundations of the earth. For me Thou didst appoint the moon for seasons and the sun knoweth his going down. For me Thou didst make every beast of the earth after his kind and every herb bearing seed and every tree in which is the fruit of a tree. For me prophet wrote and psalmist sang. For me holy men spake as they were moved by the Holy Ghost. For me Christ died, and the redemptive benefits of that death are by the miracle of His present life perpetuated forever, as efficacious now as on the day He bowed His head and gave up the ghost. And when He arose the third day it was for me; and when He poured out upon the disciples the promised Holy Spirit it was that He might continue *in me* the work He had been doing *for me* since the morning of the creation" (A. W. Tozer, *The Divine Conquest* [Camp Hill, Pa.: Christian Publications, 1978], p. 30).

Since God has done all this *for me,* I try to imagine what it would be like to be a character in each Bible story. How would I react in that situation? I ask God to show me just what it was that He was doing for me in a particular story or passage. The concept is so new to me that I have much yet to learn about applying it to my Bible reading. But I know that it has exciting possibilities.

The Bible records many intense prayers by biblical characters. When I come across them in my Bible reading—or turn to them deliberately in my need—I pray their prayers as my very own.

"When we let the Bible become our prayer, we are praying an inspired vocabulary. It will often release deep inner feelings far better than extemporized prayers that will come from our minds. God's Word is '. . . living and powerful, and sharper than any two-edged sword, piercing even to the division of soul and spirit, and of joints and marrow, and is a discerner of the thoughts and intents of the heart' (Heb. 4:12, NKJV). That which can discern and divide can certainly describe. Therefore, when used as the vehicle of our prayers, the Word of God is capable of declaring deep inner desires and thoughts of the soul-spirit" (Judson Cornwall, *Praying the Scripture* [Lake Mary, Fla.: Creation House, 1990], p. 11).

Daniel's prayer (Dan. 9) has become my prayer for my family as I intercede for them just as the prophet interceded for his people Israel. I pray along with David in the Psalms, and in the New Testament I join Jesus, the disciples, and then Paul and the other writers in their prayers and praise. Many portions of the Bible originally not intended as prayers can very well be turned into prayers. Every promise can be made a prayer. Often I am impressed that the verse I am reading speaks exactly to my need, and I ask God to fulfill that promise for me.

As I read the Bible I look for opportunities to praise and thank God whenever I recognize His hand in altering human lives and events. The Israelites never forgot the miracles that

God worked for them as He led them out of Egypt. Those miracles are still praiseworthy today—and remember, He worked those miracles for *you and me* as well as for Israel. Let's praise the Lord that He revealed His power on behalf of His children.

We often consider the stories of Daniel and the lions' den and David and Goliath as just for children. But I praise God for those miracles, too. When we sing the song of Moses and the Lamb on the sea of glass in the New Jerusalem, we will be praising Him for His miracles on behalf of humanity throughout all time. I want to be ready to join that chorus. To practice for that cosmic concert, I seek to become *involved* in the stories or passages I am reading, realizing that they are not just narratives or philosophical ideas but true accounts of how God relates Himself to His people.

I accept the admonitions and warnings the Bible presents. Often God uses them to show me my own weaknesses and sins. Then I ask Him for forgiveness and healing. Whenever in my Bible reading I run across an opportunity to rededicate my life to Him, *I do so!*

As we read the Bible this way it is impossible to separate our prayertime and our studytime. The concepts gained in active Bible reading will permeate our lives and change us.

Reading a variety of versions and translations is another way to enlarge our thinking and keep Bible reading fresh and interesting. This generation has been especially blessed with the advent of modern versions of the Bible. Although I still love the cadence and majesty of the King James Version, yet I have to admit that the language of A.D. 1611 is really not the same one I speak today. Because I was always a lover of storybooks and fantasy as a child, I often read the Bible in the same way. It was beautiful but not real. The down-to-earth language of the newer versions has blessed me with a greater sense of God's reality.

Of course, I grew up with the King James Version of the Bible, as did all my generation. My parents often read Scripture aloud to us at worship time. I am grateful for this exposure to the beauty of God's Word. We loved the Bible stories and just listened to the rest, lulled by the tones of our father's voice as he

read. I especially remember enjoying the Psalms. One of our fa-
vorites—and one we all memorized—was the twenty-third
psalm. Talk about beauty! Even as a child I appreciated its
majesty and cadence. But I enjoyed it solely for its beauty and
its comfort, and sensed no practical application to my life. For
instance, "He leadeth me in the paths of righteousness for his
name's sake." What paths are those? As a child I just imagined
them as pleasant sunlit paths that led to God. And because I had
learned that verse as a child, I was never challenged as an adult
to look at it in a fresh way. Until I discovered a new rendition of
the psalm, that is.

One day soon after the publication of *The Living Bible* I decided to memorize its paraphrased version of Psalm 23 just for
variety. When I came to the line about paths of righteousness, I
read, "He helps me do what honors him the most." Suddenly
that verse applied to my life. I heard the voice of God speaking
to me. *Do I honor God with my actions, my words?* I wondered.
For weeks that verse rang in my mind, and I often asked before
I spoke or acted, Will this honor God? The twenty-third psalm
had become alive for me.

Another time I was delighted with the Beatitudes in the
Good News Bible. I really enjoyed the way they each began
"Happy are those" in place of the familiar "Blessed are [those]."
I understood happiness much better than blessedness. But the
one that spoke to my heart was the fourth Beatitude (Matt. 5:6).
The King James Version reads, "Blessed are they which do
hunger and thirst after righteousness: for they shall be filled."
The Good News Version says, "Happy are those whose greatest
desire is to do what the Lord requires; God will satisfy them
fully." It immediately startled me. Is my greatest desire to do
what the Lord requires? How do I feel about requirements? Do I
desire them with all my heart? The translation started me thinking a new way. I prayed to God to give me a change of heart so
that I would truly desire to do His requirements.

When I became bogged down in trying to understand
Hebrews 9, I read every version of the Bible in our personal library. *The New English Bible* straightened up my understanding

beautifully by translating the Greek term *ta hagia* with the single English word "sanctuary" each time it appeared rather than using a variety of English words as most of the versions do.

In order to keep my mind stirred up to new thoughts, it helps me to read several versions of the Bible and even a paraphrase such as *The Living Bible.* You see, we are all individuals. We don't all come to conclusions in the same way. Different words have different meanings to some of us. Reading a variety of versions allows my mind to explore new thoughts.

Besides reading new versions of the Bible, it sometimes helps me to approach the Bible with new questions in mind. As an example, I remember the time I took a correspondence course through the Pacific Union Conference Education Department called Biblical Theology. The class asked me to read through each book of the Bible with one question in mind: What picture of God do I find in this book? Then I was to listen to a tape by Dr. Graham Maxwell discussing the book I was reading, and write a short one-page paper answering that question. Since I had just received my first copy of the New International Version of the Bible, I read it for that class. It was astonishing to me to see how that single question, applied to each book, opened up new areas of thought. It was while I was reading the Bible to answer that question that the Holy Spirit impressed upon me how very much God desires a personal relationship—an intimate family relationship—with each of us. And it was through looking for the picture of God that I began to see the whole Bible as a connected story of the plan of salvation—God's everlasting covenant made between earth and heaven.

You can use the Sabbath school lessons dealing with individual books of the Bible in much the same way to search for a new picture of God. The apostle Paul urged the young Timothy to "stir up" (KJV) or "fan into flame" (NIV) the gift of the Spirit given him (2 Tim. 1:6). I have needed to learn to do the same, consciously stirring up my mind to think new thoughts.

Another way I have found to increase my sensitivity to God's voice in my own life is in learning lists. Now before you assure me that you are not a person who makes out lists to live by, let me tell you that neither am I! These are not my lists but ones I have found in the Bible or the writings of Ellen White. By memorizing them I have an *outline* stored in my mind so that wherever I am I can recall them and meditate on what God wants to teach me from such God-given lists. They are handy for times I find myself waiting somewhere with nothing to do—in the doctor's office, in the car, wherever. They are even useful for sleepless hours in the night or when I am too tired to read. I can sit back by the fire and meditate. (Perhaps my years of daydreaming were good practice for something after all!) Also, such lists are a good basis for in-depth Bible study as I look up verses about each item in the list and contrast and compare them.

My favorite list is that of the fruit the Holy Spirit promises to produce in my life: love, joy, peace, patience, kindness, goodness, faithfulness, gentleness, and self-control (Gal. 5:22, 23). Every day I ask the Lord to make Himself visible in me through these attributes, so that others can see Him in my life. Often I remind Him that He has promised that I will be like a tree growing by a river producing fruit in season, and whose leaves will never wither (Ps. 1:3). The exciting thing about such a list is the possibilities both for investigating Scripture and for contemplation.

Another list that goes right along with the fruit of the Spirit is that of the aspects of the Holy Spirit found in Isaiah 11:1-5. There God lists the ways the Spirit would rest on Jesus, the Branch, when He came to earth as a man. This may be one you are unfamiliar with, but it is a blessing to me daily as I ask God to fill me with wisdom, understanding, counsel, power, knowledge, fear of the Lord, and righteous judgment. How I need such attributes! God has promised the Holy Spirit to each of us as we ask for Him. The list in Isaiah 11 helps me to begin to understand just what it is the Holy Spirit will do for me, the ways He will work in my life.

The armor of God is a more familiar list. Every morning I tell God that it is my desire to wear His armor that day (Eph. 6:10-18). One morning I was feeling sorrow for some failure of mine the day before, and as I talked with God about the armor, I asked

Him how in the world my faith was ever going to be strong enough to protect me from falling. Later that same morning as I was walking I reviewed Psalm 91. When I came to the words "his faithfulness will be your shield and rampart," a light burst upon me.

"His faithfulness, not mine," I exclaimed. "Of course. Why haven't I realized that before? My faithfulness can never be my armor. It is *God's faithfulness* that protects me!" I praised God right there as I walked those city streets.

Another morning as I asked God to fit my feet with the readiness of the gospel of peace, it came to me that Jesus wore that readiness of the gospel of peace upon His feet every day of His life on earth. His earthly sandals took Him all over His small Jewish world to spread peace, which eventually will fill the whole universe.

"O Father," I prayed, "fit my feet with the very same sandals Jesus wore, that I may cheerfully go where You want me to go today."

You might also consider Paul's list of what to think about (Phil. 4:8) and Peter's list of how to be a productive Christian (2 Peter 1:5-7). In addition, you will find many short two-part lists such as James's counsel on how to keep unspotted from the world (James 1:27) and Jesus' blessing to those who hear and obey God's Word (Luke 11:28).

I have even discovered lists that encompass whole books of the Bible, such as the book of Hebrews. Someone once pointed out to me that the theme of the book of Hebrews is "something better." Each chapter then shows us how God has given us something better in Christ than anything the world can offer. Here's the list: A better One to worship, chapter 1; a better humanity, chapter 2; a better Sonship, chapter 3; a better rest, chapter 4; a better ordination, chapter 5; a better oath and a better hope, chapter 6; a better priesthood, chapter 7; a better ministry and covenant, chapter 8; a better sanctuary and mediation, chapter 9; a better sacrifice, chapter 10; a better country and city, chapter 11; better discipline, chapter 12. Although I have not memorized this list yet, I have clearly marked the chapters in the book of Hebrews in my Bible with these captions, and they aid me in my Bible study.

One of my favorite short two-part lists is not from the Bible and I do not remember where I found it, but it is worth remembering: There are two senses we need to keep sharp. One is the sense of the sinfulness of sin, and the other a sense of the presence of God. I am often blessed and benefited by remembering that statement.

Another list that continually benefits me comes from *Steps to Christ,* page 71. Ellen White mentions four things that Satan uses to separate us from God: (1) the pleasures of this world; (2) life's cares, perplexities, and sorrows; (3) the faults of others; (4) our own faults and imperfections. I often use this list to check myself to see if I am allowing any of them to separate me from my trust in God.

My husband showed me a short list from *The Desire of Ages* the other day: "[1] *Love for God,* [2] *zeal for His glory,* and [3] *love for fallen humanity* brought Jesus to earth to suffer and to die. This was the controlling power of His life. This principle He bids us adopt" (p. 330).

If this is a principle God wants us to adopt, it's worth memorizing and meditating upon. My prayer response is "Lord, help me to love You supremely, produce in me zeal for Your glory, and may I love fallen humanity as You do. Since this principle brought Jesus to earth to die for me, may it also be the controlling principle of my life."

Lists? Well, maybe a strange way to cultivate hearing the voice of God. But it works for me.

By now you've gotten the idea. I'm sure you can find many more lists of your own. Perhaps, like me, you're eager to use any tool that fastens the things of God in your mind and gives Him another opportunity to speak to you.

The only way I have found to keep a continual sense of the presence of God in my life is to fill my mind with heavenly thoughts. Active Bible reading and study, memorization, contemplation of lists—all these have aided me in *learning to listen.*

Summary

Since a sense of the presence of God has a direct relationship to our faith, and faith comes by hearing God's Word, the more involved we become in Scripture, the greater will be our sense of His presence and our ability to hear His voice.

Each of us has a part to play in making God's Word real to us. We must *choose* to make Scripture an important part of our lives and then act upon that choice.

Ways I deliberately involve myself with Scripture:

1. Memorizing scripture.
2. Topical study of the Bible, comparing text with text.
3. *Active* Bible reading, remembering that God's Word is just as creative today as it was when He created the world:
   a. I ask God to show me how this verse or passage applies to me.
   b. I pray the prayers I find in the Bible—or put appropriate scriptures into a personal prayer.
   c. I look for opportunities to praise God—for His miracles and for His love.
   d. I accept the admonitions and warnings the Bible presents. Often God uses them to show me my own weaknesses and sins. I ask God for forgiveness and healing.
   e. Whenever I find an opportunity to rededicate my life to God during my Bible reading, *I do so!*
4. I read the Bible in different versions.
5. I read the Bible with a specific question in mind, such as, What is the picture of God I find in this passage?
6. I memorize the lists that I find in the Bible or writings of Ellen White and meditate on them.

These methods of familiarizing my mind with Scripture give God opportunities to speak with me continually.

CHAPTER SEVEN

Life Is a Parable

*L*earning to listen to the voice of God is a matter of cultivating the proper atmosphere for hearing it. I have
devoted several chapters relating the different ways that God has
made Scripture real to me, how He speaks through its words as
He applies them to my particular circumstances. But God has
other ways of speaking, too.

One of them is through physical work. God does not want
to make us so "heavenly minded that we are no earthly good."
Jesus showed us by His parables how to combine spiritual
lessons and daily work. By mingling His teachings with references to farming and fishing, raising a family, and cleaning a
house, Jesus made sure that we would daily remember His
lessons. He spoke of cultivating vineyards and managing an es-
tate; of servants and masters, fathers and sons. His stories
reached the highest and the lowest classes of people. As human
beings we all have basic physical activities each day. If we can
learn to inject spiritual lessons into our daily work, it will greatly
increase our ability to hear God's voice.

A few years ago God taught me this lesson. I was just beginning to explore the deep things of God and was frustrated by
being continually tied down to housekeeping. Longing to spend
hours in Bible study and prayer, I craved intellectual conversation and stimulation. But what occupied my time? Housecleaning, cooking, washing, ironing, and child care for four
preadolescents. Plus, of course, the responsibilities of being a

pastor's wife. Naturally I chaffed a bit at the restrictions.

God continually surprises me. He didn't tell me to shape up, get to work, and stop dreaming. No, God began showing me that one of His best lesson books is physical labor. The lessons He taught me changed my attitude toward housecleaning, dishes, ironing, and all such daily work for all time.

I can't actually explain how God spoke to me. All I know is that as I washed the dishes I began to realize that my life was as soiled as the plate in my hand, but that God would wash me clean in living water straight from the throne of God. My time at the kitchen sink became a session of communion with God. In fact, the presence of God filled my whole house!

The kitchen and family room floors were asphalt tile and seemed to attract black marks like a magnet draws metal. I spent hours every week on my knees cleaning the floors. But God knelt with me, and as I scrubbed up the black marks on my floor He told me that His forgiveness could erase every black mark in my life.

Ironing became one of my favorite occupations, for God assured me that He would not only iron out the wrinkles in my own life but would do it for my children, too! I prayed especially for the child whose clothes I was ironing, and I tucked God's love in all the pockets.

God took from me the restlessness for bigger, greater service and learning, and left me content with the work He had given me. I hadn't even realized that it was what I needed. But He knew. With my "happy ever after" mentality I believed that I would always walk and talk in this special way with God. But my time of daily closeness and teaching by God lasted only about six weeks. After that I would often have days when the same Presence returned, in the same way, but not continually. Still those weeks of special training had lasting results. I never forgot the lessons I learned, and my appreciation of housekeeping became permanent.

God gave me a special gift those few weeks, though it was not something that I had specifically asked Him for or that I planned for. But I feel that it is possible to cultivate this type of spiritual awareness in the daily duties of life and thus have a greater sense of His presence. I believe that God wants us to enjoy the necessary labor of life, be it housework, gardening, janitor work, carpentry, auto mechanics, cooking, or the daily care of children. We may call them mundane tasks, but with the presence of Jesus they can be an opportunity to hear His voice. God has done this often for me since then.

One Friday morning several months after I began finding housework a time of spiritual blessing, I talked with God about how thrilled I was about all that He was teaching me. I had just begun working away from home four days a week, and Friday was my only weekday at home.

"Today, Lord," I said that morning, "I'm going to be cleaning house, washing clothes, and cooking in preparation for the Sabbath. I want to have my mind tuned into You in every thing I do. I want to learn special lessons from all that I do today. Let's make this a perfect Friday!"

Eager to begin a day of discovery, I descended the stairs from my bedroom with a song in my heart. As I neared the foot of the stairs I heard our Siamese cat, Samantha, crying at the family room sliding glass door and wanting to be let in. Quickly crossing the room, I slid open the glass door with my left hand and reached for the screen door with my right hand. I am naturally quick in all my movements and was especially so that morning, as I was eager to begin an exciting day. What I had forgotten in my haste was that the screen door had been sticking lately. So as I tugged at the screen I gasped in surprise and pain. Holding up my right hand, I gazed in horror at my finger. The fingernail was torn back into the quick of the nail. Samantha was sidling around my ankles, but I ignored her.

"God," I exclaimed out loud, "how could You have let this happen today? Look at my finger. It's going to hurt all day. How can I think about You when my finger hurts so bad? If I put a bandage around it, it will fall off in the water as I clean bathtubs and showers and wash dishes. But if I don't, the loose nail will catch on everything. And it will hurt! Oh, how could You have let this happen on this day that was to have been my perfect

Friday? I was going to learn so much. Now I will just hurt."

Sometimes I have to wait to hear God's answers. But this time He answered immediately.

"Carrol," God said, "every time your finger hurts today, just remember how very much I love you."

And so I began my Friday. I was right about the pain and the bandage. I started off with a bandage, even replaced it a couple of times, then finally gave up and went on without it. And my torn nail caught on everything just as I had predicted. But every time pain crossed my consciousness—and that was often!—I remembered, "God loves me *so much!*"

As Friday ended and the Sabbath began, my family gathered around the dining-room table for worship and supper. As I sliced the still-warm banana nut bread I recalled my day. How blessed I had been! I had planned a perfect Friday with God teaching me numerous exciting truths. But He had known that I needed to learn *one* basic lesson—that God loved me no matter what trial I had to face. All day long I had heard Him say, "I love you. I love you. I will *always* love you." It had truly been a perfect Friday as my hurt finger constantly drew my wandering mind to God.

Not only does God want to teach us to combine spiritual lessons with our work, but He plans for us to teach our children by the same methods.

Not long after my experience with the torn fingernail, my daughter, Julie, and I went grocery shopping one Friday afternoon. As we bought groceries we succumbed to a "special"—a set of dishes—at our supermarket. While we put away the groceries we also looked for room in our already crowded cupboards to put away the new dishes. One of the set's attractions for me was the eight lovely green soup bowls.

As I was gloating over the shining newness of the green bowls Julie probed my silence with the question "These old blue bowls—we'll keep them even though we have these new ones, won't we?"

I turned from my admiration of the new bowls to look at the blue ones in Julie's hands. Suddenly they seemed to mirror the past: hot buttered popcorn on Saturday nights, steaming vegetable stew on cold winter evenings, creamy cooked cereal in the early-morning hours before school, homemade peach ice-cream on summer evenings. I was smiling at the happy memories the blue bowls brought when her gentle voice again broke the silence.

"I remember that Dad taught me about God from these blue bowls."

"About God?" I asked in amazement. "From these blue bowls?" I took one in my hand.

"Yes," she mused. "I couldn't understand how God could be everlasting—no beginning and no end. We were eating, and Dad pointed to the rim of my bowl. 'Where is the beginning and where is the end of the rim of the bowl?' he asked. So every time I've puzzled about God's existence I've remembered the blue bowls."

I believe that it is God's desire to link knowledge of Him to everything in our homes. That way our children will glimpse truth wherever they look, whatever they do.

Yes, life is a parable. It is God's plan that everything around us add to our understanding of Him. If we are truly seeking Him, He will illumine ordinary events and ordinary things so that we can catch glimpses of Him in nature, in human relations, and in all of life's circumstances. He will speak to us in tones we cannot mistake, saying, "No, I'm not like that," or "Yes, this is what I'm like." It's really not surprising that He would appear especially in the work world. He assigned labor to Adam and Eve in the Garden of Eden even before the entrance of sin. Physical work is a blessing, giving us mental, physical, and spiritual health.

Life is a parable. The one who has learned to listen will hear the voice of God and rejoice.

Summary

One of the ways God speaks to us is through physical work. Jesus illustrated His teaching by stories about daily life. If we can learn to combine spiritual lessons with our daily work, it will greatly increase our ability to hear His voice.

Not only does God teach us individually from daily work, but He desires that we instruct our children about Him in the same way so that wherever they look, wherever they go, they will be constantly reminded of Him.

If we have ears to hear the voice of the Holy Spirit, God will illumine ordinary events and ordinary things so that we can catch glimpses of Him in nature, in human relations, and in life's circumstances.

God gave Adam and Eve their work *before* sin entered. Physical work is a blessing, giving us mental, physical, and spiritual health.

Yes, life is a parable.

CHAPTER EIGHT

Learning to Speak Our Native Language

$\mathcal{G}$od's wonderful plan for all humanity was that they would be His children, basking in an intimate family relationship with Him. It was His plan before sin entered, and it is still His plan, thanks to Jesus. When we accept Him as our Saviour, we immediately receive the gift of sonship by the Holy Spirit. Walking in the Spirit is the normal life of the Christian. Hearing the inner voice of God is the birthright of God's sons and daughters.

But sometimes we forget that wonderful privilege. Or some of us have never discovered that the desires in our hearts toward God are His voice speaking to us. But it is true. Any yearning we feel toward God or any reaching out toward Him is the wooing and drawing of the Holy Spirit. We cannot live spiritually without the inner voice of God. Always we should cherish that voice, carefully listening when He speaks, and responding by pouring out our hearts to Him in love, gratitude, and praise. King David shows us how to be receptive to God's reaching out for us in what I call the "yearning" verses:

"O God, you are my God,
earnestly I seek you;
my soul thirsts for you,
my body longs for you,
in a dry and weary land
where there is no water" (Ps. 63:1).

"As the deer pants for streams of water,
   so my soul pants for you, O God.
   My soul thirsts for God, for the living God.
   When can I go and meet with God?" (Ps. 42:1, 2).

"How lovely is your dwelling place,
   O Lord Almighty!
   My soul yearns, even faints,
   for the courts of the Lord;
   my heart and my flesh cry out
   for the living God" (Ps. 84:1, 2).

"One thing I ask of the Lord,
   this is what I seek:
   that I may dwell in the house of the Lord
   all the days of my life,
   to gaze upon the beauty of the Lord
   and to seek him in his temple" (Ps. 27:4).

"How sweet are your words to my taste,
   sweeter than honey to my mouth!" (Ps. 119:103).

"Whom have I in heaven but you?
   And earth has nothing I desire besides you.
   My flesh and my heart may fail,
   but God is the strength of my heart
   and my portion forever" (Ps. 73:25, 26).

The prophet Isaiah adds one more:

"My soul yearns for you in the night,
   in the morning my spirit longs for you" (Isa. 26:9).

This is the kind of attitude God longs for in His children. When He reaches out to us in love, He desires a love and praise response from the very depth of our hearts. We would be far more conscious of His presence in our lives if we cultivated responses like this to the heart call of our heavenly Father. In Psalm 103 David begins:

> "Praise the Lord, O my soul;
> *all my inmost being, praise his holy name*"
> (verse 1).

God desires the love response of our inmost being. When He draws me, my heart should declare, "Oh, Lord, I desire You more than anything else in life. I can't imagine life without You. I want to please You in all that I do because I love You with all my heart." In our human relationships, when someone tells us that they love us, we usually reply, "I love you, too." How much more should we respond thus to God! Because our walk with God is a life of *faith,* not of sight, we do not need to even wait to *feel* God calling us in our emotions—rather, we can by faith *know* that He is telling us of His love. Since this is true, we can give Him our love response continually.

Although often God's inner voice points out sin in our lives or warns us from wrongdoing, yet sometimes we find God calling us into a closer love relationship with Him.

One evening my husband and I were playing our favorite word game, Changeling. It employs letter tiles like those used in Scrabble, but it is played on the table rather than on a crossword board. The object of the game is for the player to make two words out of one word on the table by adding letters from his or her own rack to make the highest possible score. That evening we had started our game rather late, and soon after we had begun I became so sleepy that I was sorry that I had said I would play. I just wanted the game to be over so I could go to bed. But I hated to mention it to my husband, who seemed to be enjoying himself.

It was my husband's turn to play, and as he put his words on the table he said, "I'm not going to make a high score from this play, but these are two *very nice words."*

I looked down and saw "loving" and "Lord." My sleepy mind awoke as if God had touched me. "Loving Lord," my heart responded. "Oh, yes, He is a loving Lord." Glancing up, I met John's smile. It was obvious that God had touched us both with His love as we played that simple game. I enjoyed the rest of the game, "He is a loving Lord" often echoing in my mind. How my heart rejoiced!

As I said my prayer that night I thanked God for being a loving Lord. Every time I awoke in the night I remembered with joy, "He is a loving Lord." Toward morning I got up to go to the bathroom and remembered again that He is my loving Lord. As I smiled in the darkness another voice intruded into my mind.

"How ridiculous it is for you to think that God spoke to you in that game that way! God doesn't speak to people in such trivial ways. That was just your own emotional response to those words. It was not God."

Immediately depression settled over me like a cloak. But then I realized, "Wait a minute, that was Satan speaking through my own doubt! I'm not going to let him destroy the joy of my relationship with Jesus." Breathing a prayer to God, I asked, "Please rebuke Satan in the name of Jesus for trying to make me doubt Your presence in my daily life." The darkness lifted. "Oh, He is a loving Lord," I exclaimed again.

The same Father who told the world "This is my beloved Son, in whom I am well pleased [Matt. 3:17, KJV]" has the same care for you and me. It's hard to believe, but it's true. Because Jesus pleased God, we, too, can please Him. We can please Him in every activity of life—in our recreation, in our work, and in our prayers. He wants to be present with us always because He is our Loving Lord.

Every time I remember that evening, that game, and that encounter, I smile as I cry anew, "He is my loving Lord!"

Sometimes we miss out on blessings God wants to bestow on us either because we don't realize that they are available or because we are timid or fearful. In that case a conscious step toward God may surprise us. One Wednesday evening I did not attend prayer meeting with my husband because I was not feeling well. Going to bed early, I put a couple of pillows behind my head so that I could read until I became sleepy. It depressed me a little that I had to miss out on the fellowship of prayer meeting, but I determined to seek a blessing through my reading. My book was the first volume of Arthur White's biography of Ellen White, *The Early Years.* On page 181 White quotes a letter written by his grandmother in 1850 after one of her visions. In it she mentions that the angel told her that singing and shouting to the glory of God would drive back the enemy. I was surprised, not having encountered such a statement before. Laying the book down, I thought about it. *Shouting* praise to God would drive back the enemy?

"Well, why not try it?" I asked myself. "There's no one in the house except me. If I were at prayer meeting, I would be speaking aloud my praises to God. I'll just shout them here in my bedroom."

Feeling rather foolish, I exclaimed, "Praise the Lord!" Immediately all depression left me, and I sensed the strong presence of God. I shouted some more, "O Lord, I love You and adore You. Praise Your holy name!" On and on I praised the Lord for His goodness, His blessings, and His love. Suddenly I rolled out of bed and onto my knees, still praising Him. I had my own little prayer and praise meeting right there in my bedroom.

Now, I have never shouted in a meeting, and I don't intend to! Whatever we do in praise of God must come from a sincere heart, faith and love blending together in appropriate expression. But perhaps we need to learn to put aside our timidity and be more vocal in our personal praise. We might discover that we can rout the enemy more easily than we have experienced in the past.

In the quotation I mentioned above, Ellen White mentioned shouting and *singing* praises to God as having the ability to drive back the enemy. Music is one of God's greatest gifts to humanity, and when used to praise God it brings the atmosphere of heaven into our hearts. The Bible shows us the importance of song. In Old Testament times God told the leaders of Israel to form a choir and band to lead the army into battle! Song is as much a part of our worship of God as is prayer. Jesus, when He was a man on earth, gave us His example of the use of song:

"With a song, Jesus in His earthly life met temptation. Often when sharp, stinging words were spoken, often when the atmosphere about Him was heavy with gloom, with dissatisfaction, distrust, or oppressive fear, was heard His song of faith and holy cheer" *(Education,* p. 166).

"Jesus carried into His labor cheerfulness and tact. . . . Often He expressed the gladness of His heart by singing psalms and heavenly songs. Often the dwellers in Nazareth heard His voice raised in praise and thanksgiving to God. He held communion with heaven in song; and as His companions complained of weariness from labor, they were cheered by the sweet melody from His lips. His praise seemed to banish the evil angels, and, like incense, fill the place with fragrance. The minds of His hearers were carried away from their earthly exile, to the heavenly home" *(The Desire of Ages,* p. 73).

Like Jesus, we too can always remember that "song is a weapon we can always use against discouragement" *(The Ministry of Healing,* p. 254). What a blessing it would be in our lives if we only remembered it at the right times! Even before I had ever read the statements I have quoted above, God had used music to vanquish the enemy of depression in my life.

One hot summer morning I awoke late to a house already bustling with childish activity. Hurriedly I dressed and gathered my four children and two others I was keeping into the living room for morning worship. My own personal devotions that morning had been only a hasty prayer to the background sounds of busy children. Breakfast, which immediately followed worship, was a hubbub of excited plans for another lovely summer day. My minister husband left soon for his duties, and the six children scampered off to play.

Left alone in the kitchen, I contemplated my own day. The washer was already churning its monotonous song, dirty dishes filled the sink, the beds were unmade, and I had six children to keep happy all the long hot summer day. I felt too depressed for words!

As I started the dishwater, I thought, *Oh, if I only had time to go apart and study and pray, I could shake off this depression.*

Two little Indians passing through the kitchen in their play made me realize how impossible study, quiet, and prayer were at my house that day.

As I washed dish after dish I tried to shake the feeling of depression that engulfed me.

"Dear Lord," I silently prayed, "show me the way to turn this day into a blessing. Help me to be sweet and kind. Send peace to my heart."

The way God answers prayers is so varied—who can predict how He will answer?

I fell to dreaming of days gone by when I was a little girl who loved solitude. My parents, my two sisters, and I lived on a northern California ranch with acres and acres of peace and quiet. I used to go off alone for hours into the forest of stately pines and listen to the birds sing praises to God. There I would join the birds and pour out in song my heart's longing and my love for God. They were never real "written" songs, just the overflowings of my childish heart. Yet I felt rested and relieved after such a walk and "sing."

Years had changed the uninhibited child into a modern-day woman. As I pushed my clothes cart out into the sunshine of that July day, a strange thought flashed through my mind: "Dare I sing?"

Pausing, I looked around and listened. It was amazingly quiet for our city community. No radios blaring. No one talking. Even the children seemed to have disappeared.

For a moment a gleam of the old childish "me" appeared. "All right," I answered myself, "I dare!"

I began to sing as I hung the clothes in orderly rows upon the lines. First I sang of God's goodness and greatness, of His love for *me.* Hesitant at first, I grew braver until I sang full voice out upon that city air just as the child "me" had sung in the country so many years before.

Washerload after washerload of clothes I hung out that morning as I made "a joyful noise unto the Lord." I sang of the New Jerusalem and the wonderful earth made new. I felt transported to realms of glory as I joyfully sang.

Later, preparing lunch for the hungry children, I found that my smile was genuine, that it was no problem to be sweet to the six bundles of energy slowed down only by the need to refuel.

The rest of that summer day went by in a whirl of pleasant busyness.

As I sat folding clothes in my bedroom in late afternoon I reviewed the morning. "Wasn't it nice of God to send everyone out of earshot so I could sing?" I smiled to myself.

My second son came in just then and paused to help me by folding washcloths.

"Say, Mommy," he asked suddenly, "what was the name of that song you were singing this morning?"

"Oh," I answered, surprised, "why—well, it wasn't really a song, honey. I just made it up as I worked." We both were silent for a moment. "Where were you when I was singing?" I asked.

"Oh, we were all playing at the side of the house, but when you began to sing we stopped and listened. It was pretty, Mommy."

I gulped, nonplussed.

"You know what it made me think of, Mommy, hearing you sing like that?" went on my small son.

"What?"

"Oh, that we lived *way* out in the country and a *very happy* Mommy was hanging up the clothes."

He gave me a loving smile and, having finished folding the washcloths, hastened out to play.

My eyes filled with tears. God had turned a miserable day into a memorable one.

I have found that singing hymns of praise changes the atmosphere of the home. When our children were small we sang not only at worship, morning and evening, but also in the car. But I've discovered since then that even when alone I can enjoy the sense of God's presence that singing brings. I sing in my personal prayer time. Now, I'm not a singer by any stretch of even my vivid imagination! But one doesn't have to have a gifted voice to sing for God's praise privately. You see, in God's sight even those whom we consider to have beautiful voices just cannot compare with the angels. So God doesn't check our singing by musical standards but by how much we love Him! So I sing. It lifts my spirits, and I believe that God enjoys it too. When I was a school librarian I often sang in the car on my way to work. My favorite was the little chorus "I have decided to follow Jesus, no turning back, no turning back." I sang it as a prayer, my personal recommitment to Jesus.

Singing has a freshness, a youthfulness, that I believe God appreciates. David says that even in old age we can stay "fresh and green" (Ps. 92:14). My 91-year-old mother is an example of the youthfulness that God bestows on those who reach out to Him in praise. She lives alone, still drives, and not only takes care of herself but is active in Community Services and in providing rides for her friends who no longer drive to the store for groceries or on other errands. Mother keeps a small vegetable garden, and her greatest pleasure is working in her yard among her flowers. Because we live hundreds of miles apart and only see each other face-to-face twice a year at best and often only once, I call her every Friday morning at 7:30 and we talk until 8:00 when the phone rates go up. One Friday morning I noticed that her voice was a little hoarse. Mother is not a complainer and often does not tell me when she is not feeling well, so I asked her if she had a cold.

"No," she answered, "I don't have a cold."

"Maybe your voice is hoarse because you haven't been talking much this morning," I pursued the subject.

"Well," she said, "it might be because I've been singing."

"You've been singing?" I asked, surprised.

"Yes," Mother said, rather hesitantly, "I keep a *Christ in Song* book near where I have my morning devotions, and I often sing some of the old songs for my worship. This morning I was singing 'I'm a Child of the King.'"

Tears came to my eyes as I imagined the pleasure it brings God to hear my 91-year-old mother sing.

I asked her if it would embarrass her too much if I told this story in my book. She was a little hesitant. "Anyone who knows me," she said, "knows that I can't sing!"

"I know, Mother," I explained, "and anyone who knows me knows that I can't sing, either. But the wonderful thing is that God knows that we can sing with the heart!"

So Mother agreed to let me tell her story if I would bury it deep within a chapter. So I have!

The love response to God of prayer and praise is the native language of the Christian. But some of us have almost forgotten how to speak it. Cultivating that response will help us to learn how to listen to the still, small voice of God in our hearts.

Summary

Hearing the inner voice of God is the birthright of God's sons and daughters.

We should remember that anytime we sense a drawing toward God that it is indeed Him calling us to Him. We should cherish that voice, tenderly listening when He speaks and responding in expressions of love, gratitude, and praise. Since we walk by *faith,* not sight, we can know by faith that God is continually wooing us to Himself. Thus we do not have to wait for an emotional drawing in order to respond to Him.

God desires the love response of our inmost being. We will be blessed by a vocal response, either in the words of Scripture, such as that of David in the Psalms, or by telling Him in our own words how much we love and adore Him and desire to please Him. (The Psalms give us many examples of this type of love response. Psalm 63:1; 42:1, 2; 84:1, 2; 27:4; 119:103; 73:25, 26 are just a few.)

A *vocal,* either shouted or sung, praise to God is powerful for driving back the power of the enemy.

The love response to God of prayer and praise is the native language of the Christian.

CHAPTER NINE

What Can I Expect God to Talk About?

*W*e hear a lot of predictions these days claiming to come from a supernatural source. Sensational magazines devote pages at the beginning of every year to predictions of what will happen to movie and TV stars and other celebrities, along with national and international events, during the coming months. Although they may have a supernatural source, they are not from God. God's interest is in the outworking of the plan of redemption. He is concerned with the salvation of human beings. When He speaks to us, He presents things of eternal consequences. And it is unlikely that He will ever tell me about someone else's future. After Jesus had revealed to Peter how he would die, the disciple asked, "What about John? What's going to happen to him?" Jesus replied, "If I want him to remain alive until I return, what is that to you? You must follow me" (John 21:22).

Because God does not speak loudly but in the inward voice of the Holy Spirit to our hearts, it is easy amid the clamor of the world around us to miss His words. What can we expect God to talk about? The answer to this question may help us distinguish His voice from that of a counterfeit.

We know He isn't going to reveal things about movie stars or politicians. But what topics is He interested in? Is He actually concerned about my personal affairs?

Jesus' disciples had many of the same questions. When He told them that He was leaving them to go to the Father, Philip asked Him to show them the Father. "Anyone who has seen me," Jesus replied, "has seen the Father" (John 14:9).

As we read the Bible account of the life of Jesus we find that He always focused on what concerned His disciples. He worked a miracle to find a coin so that Peter could pay the temple tax, and provided food for the hungry 5,000. So we can know that God will talk to us about just such personal items. In fact, everything that we bring to Him in prayer He will in some manner respond to.

As we become less self-centered and discuss with Him more about the needs of others, He will speak to us about ways that we can help them. But He will never reveal to us the personal matters of others and intrude upon their privacy. Jesus, in dealing with the men who had led the woman into adultery, did not disclose their sins to the crowd. By writing them upon the ground He revealed to each one His knowledge of their sin but did not disclose it beyond that.

Pastors and other church workers, concerned elders and friends, may sometimes need to confront someone because of his or her sin. In such cases we can expect that God will direct us through the inward voice of the Spirit as to how to deal with the person. Ellen White counseled us, "Not until you feel that you could sacrifice your own self-dignity, and even lay down your life in order to save an erring brother, have you cast the beam out of your own eye so that you are prepared to help your brother. Then you can approach him and touch his heart. No one has ever been reclaimed from a wrong position by censure and reproach; but many have thus been driven from Christ and led to seal their hearts against conviction. A tender spirit, a gentle, winning deportment, may save the erring and hide a multitude of sins" (Thoughts From the Mount of Blessing, pp. 128, 129).

The apostle Paul advised us, "Brothers, if someone is caught in a sin, you who are spiritual should restore him gently. But watch yourself, or you may be tempted. Carry each other's burdens, and in this way you will fulfill the law of Christ" (Gal. 6:1, 2).

We should never undertake the work of restoration from sin carelessly. Only the direction of the Holy Spirit and a spirit of humility and prayer can enable us to reach out and touch a sinner.

But what about the simple little things, you may ask, that are a trial to me? Will God talk to me about those? Things like diet, houses, clothes, jobs, children, relationships?

Always remember that God is our Father and *anything* that concerns us—anything that is a part of our lives—He is interested in. I mentioned in the preceding chapters how God involved Himself even in my work. Nothing is beneath His notice. Jesus told us that the Father is aware of even the little sparrow that falls to the ground. How much more He cares for all our worries and concerns.

God is interested in even the clothes we wear! He has given us sound principles for wearing good quality, modest, simple but attractive, clothing. But I believe He is able and willing to guide us in our individual selection of clothes today.

I have long had a problem with finding comfortable shoes. My feet appear perfectly normal. But I cannot find comfortable shoes. I have wasted hundreds of dollars over the past 45 years on shoes that I simply could not wear! It isn't as though I have tried to wear inexpensive shoes, either. I have known that only the best shoes would possibly fit my feet. So I've searched out lovely shoes that looked comfortable and even felt comfortable to me in the store. And inevitably they have been very expensive. Yet after a few hours on my feet I knew that I could never wear them again.

Although I had talked to the Lord about this problem before, finally one day I came to my wit's end.

"I've wasted enough money on shoes, Father," I said. "It's time that I use that money for something more profitable. And besides, I *need* comfortable shoes. How can I stand up to speak for You when my feet hurt? Someway, somehow, Lord, it's time for me to find a way to buy comfortable shoes."

I was a little concerned as my last pair of dress shoes suitable for seminars was beginning to look rather shabby. To be truthful, they weren't really comfortable either, but they were the best I had. How was I going to find a new pair? Asking God for guidance and direction, I reminded Him that I needed shoes in order to go about His business.

The subject of shoes remained on my mind. A few days later I was talking to a friend on the telephone and somehow I mentioned my concern about finding some comfortable shoes to lecture in. "I'm tired of wasting money on shoes I can't wear," I said. "I've asked God to give me some comfortable shoes."

My friend chuckled. "I know," she said, "I have trouble with my feet too, but I've found a shoe store that deals in hard-to-fit feet."

"What's the address?" I asked. "Is it around here?"

The next day I drove over to the little shop. Big sale signs filled the windows. Hopeful, I looked over the merchandise and found several attractive styles, both in dress shoes and casual shoes. The sale prices were great. I tried them on, growing excited as I found them comfortable. But then, I reminded myself, shoes often felt good in the store but turned out to be a different story when I arrived home.

"Well?" asked the expectant clerk, "which ones are you going to take?" I wanted to tell her to go away so that I could pray, but I just said I'd have to think about it a little more. Taking a seat, I stared at the shoes. "Lord," I prayed silently, "is this Your answer to my prayer? Or am I just going to waste more money?" I would have loved it if God had spoken directly to me in words right in that shoe store, telling me that they were the shoes He had chosen for me. But sometimes God speaks through providences, wanting to build our faith. After all, I had prayed and a friend had told me about the store. Never before had I felt directed to a special store. Surely it all had to be God's leading. Deciding to go ahead on faith, I bought four pairs of shoes—two pairs of dress shoes and two for casual use.

When I came home with my bag of shoes my husband raised his eyebrows. He was well acquainted with my relationship with shoes. (No wonder I go barefoot at home most of the time.) But the delightful thing this time was that every pair I bought that day turned out to be comfortable! I still wear some of them. Since that day I have purchased two more pairs of serviceable dress shoes from that same store—all wearable.

I'm so glad that God is interested in talking to me about shoes.

In just the same way God will help us in making choices about careers, cars, homes, and finances. He wants to be involved in our business transactions, our living and eating habits and styles. God wants us to counsel with Him about our marriages, our child rearing.

But above and beyond all these things, God has one thing He wants us to keep in mind: "Seek first his kingdom and his righteousness, and all these things will be given you as well" (Matt. 6:33). Jesus made this comment right after He had been talking about the physical necessities of life. So it's obvious that He considered such things secondary to our desire for His kingdom.

The apostle Paul counseled the Corinthians: "What I mean, brothers, is that the time is short. From now on those who have wives should live as if they had none; those who mourn, as if they did not; those who are happy, as if they were not; *those who buy something, as if it were not theirs to keep; those who use the things of the world, as if not engrossed in them.* For this world in its present form is passing away. . . . I am saying this for your own good, not to restrict you, but that you may live in a right way in *undivided devotion* to the Lord" (1 Cor. 7:29-35).

How much closer we are to the time of the end than were the Corinthians!

Yes, God wants to talk to us about our personal lives and physical necessities. But even more He wants to share with us the secrets of His kingdom.

We can expect that the very same things that Jesus discussed when He lived on earth as a human being will be what God will speak to us about now. Notice that Scripture does not present God revealing great scientific discoveries or appealing to the intellectual mind. "He said nothing to gratify curiosity or to stimulate selfish ambition. He did not deal in abstract theories, but in that which is *essential to the development of character; that which will enlarge man's capacity for knowing God, and increase his power to do good.* He spoke of those truths that relate to the *conduct of life* and that *unite man with eternity"* *(Education,* p. 81; italics supplied).

Many of Christ's talks centered on the contrasts between the principles of the kingdom of heaven and those of the kingdoms of this world. When His disciples asked Him why He spoke to the people in parables, Jesus answered, "The knowledge of the secrets of the kingdom of heaven has been given to you, but not to them" (Matt. 13:11). Jesus was able to speak plainly of the kingdom of heaven with His disciples while He hid truth in parables, for the majority of the people were not able to understand spiritual things. Yet even today we learn best by hearing the parables. In them truth can grow, expand, and change as we mature spiritually. God has given the secrets of His kingdom to all who are spiritually minded.

Just before Jesus died He tried to prepare His disciples, who had been used to hearing His familiar voice, to listen for that same voice inwardly: "I will ask the Father, and he will give you another Counselor to be with you forever—the Spirit of truth. The world cannot accept him, because it neither sees him nor knows him. But you know him, for he lives with you and will be in you. I will not leave you as orphans; I will come to you. Before long, the world will not see me anymore, but you will see me. Because I live, you also will live. On that day you will realize that I am in my Father, and you are in me, and I am in you. Whoever has my commands and obeys them, he is the one who loves me. He who loves me will be loved by my Father, and I too will love him and show myself to him" (John 14:16-21).

Jesus explained this even plainer: "But the Counselor, the Holy Spirit, whom the Father will send in my name, will teach you all things and will remind you of everything I have said to you" (verse 26).

Later on in the same discourse, Jesus told the disciples that the Holy Spirit has three important subjects He will especially impress upon the hearts of all who have ears to hear spiritual things. The Spirit will bring *conviction of sin,* He will *reveal the righteousness of Christ,* and He will *warn of the coming judgment* (John 16:8-11). We can expect that God will discuss these things with us, too. In fact, the very first evidence that the Holy Spirit is speaking to us is the deep conviction that we are sinners. As we view the righteousness of Christ and accept His forgiveness, disclosed to us by the Holy Spirit, we are able to trust Him for salvation and begin that intimate family relationship we have been talking about.

Understanding that God will talk about such things with us can guide and protect us from the enemy as we listen for God's voice. Since 1844 God's people have lived in the day of judgment. It's now or never to learn about prophecy and doctrine. Today is our time to glorify God's name before the world. Now is the time to discover how to properly worship God in Sabbath observance, in commandment keeping, and in our witnessing. Now is the time to reveal Christ to the world through our relationships with those around us, to live godly lives. God wants to talk to us about the special duties and privileges He has for His last-day people. It is our privilege to walk with God as did Enoch.

God will speak to us about anything that a father, lover, or friend would. But remember that God is ever leading us to think deeper thoughts, to grow, to become the people He knows we can become in His strength. Talking with God will *always* change us.

> "But blessed is the man [or woman] who
>   trusts in the Lord,
>   whose confidence is in him.
> He [or she] will be like a tree planted by the water
>   that sends out its roots by the stream.
> It does not fear when heat comes;
>   its leaves are always green.
> It has no worries in a year of drought
> and *never fails to bear fruit"* (Jer. 17:7, 8).

We too will bear fruit when we learn to listen to God's voice.

Summary

What can I expect God to talk to me about?

He will *not* discuss movie stars or politicians with me.

But He will speak to us about anything that concerns our peace. He wants to be a part of every aspect of our lives. Even the details of our life are important to Him.

Jesus told His disciples to seek *first the kingdom of God, and everything else in life would be added.* While He knows that we must live in this world, He counsels us not to become engrossed in worldly things but to live in *undivided devotion to God.* He will talk to us about the kind of topics that Jesus presented while on earth:

Things essential to development of character.

Things that will enlarge our capacity for knowing God.

Things that will increase our power to do good.

Things that relate to the conduct of life and that unite us with eternity *(Education,* p. 81).

Also, Jesus promised His disciples that after He left them the Father would send them another Comforter, the Holy Spirit, who would always be with them and *in them.* The Holy Spirit would teach them and remind them of what Jesus had taught them.

Jesus told His disciples that the Spirit would present three important subjects:

He would convict of sin.

He would reveal the righteousness of Christ.

He would warn of the coming judgment (John 16:8-11).

God desires to lead us deeper and deeper into wisdom and knowledge of His kingdom: worship, commandment keeping, witnessing, doctrine, and prophecy.

We will always be changed as we learn to listen to the voice of God.

CHAPTER TEN

Obedience

As in any relationship, how we respond to God when He speaks to us determines how the relationship continues. Every time God communicates to us it is important that we respond. Sometimes the appropriate reaction is praise, as I have enlarged upon in chapter eight. Other times it will be repentance from sin, and sometimes action. Not responding will almost certainly lessen my future ability to hear God's voice and to sense His presence.

When God impresses me with some change I need to make in my life or something I should do, if I willingly obey I will continue to hear His voice. Putting into practice what I am learning from Bible study and prayer always *increases* my ability to recognize His words. But if I do not obey, either out of fear, rebellion, or disinterest, the conviction fades, and I am left in depression, darkness, or lukewarmness. Often it is quite a while before I again have the sense of God's presence and hear His inward voice again. A sad commentary is that often we do not even notice its absence. Disobedience deadens the conscience and will eventually lead to bitterness and disillusionment.

Fortunately our God is very patient and very gracious. When He finds a problem area in our life, He will approach it from all angles until we, too, can see it clearly and obey.

Some incidents from my own life will illustrate how God works individually. I am so grateful that the Bible stories show both failure and success. The failures give me hope for my weak self, and the successes reveal God's power. I'll share both kinds from my own experience.

You remember the story I told in chapter two of how God awakened me every morning to talk with Him. I walked with the Lord in joy as every day He worked that miracle anew for me. He talked with me as I went about my daily work.

As a background for the next part of this story I must tell you a bit more about myself. One of my personality traits is that I am a dreamer. Early in my childhood I discovered that I could use my imagination to make life more pleasant by making up stories in my head to pass away the time. As a result I was seldom bored, for I always had my imagination for company. I believe imagination is from God, and I am very grateful for the joy it brings me in my Christian walk. However, we can pervert most good things for selfish gratification—and sometimes we do it in ways that seem quite innocent.

As a child when life was unpleasant or tedious I could always retreat into my daydreams. This made me a quiet and contented child. Although I was often sick, I was uncomplaining. My imagination made paper dolls great fun for both me and my sisters. I made up the stories that our dolls lived out. Also, I told stories to my sisters after we were in bed for the night. Each tale continued nightly for a week or more. Even I didn't know from day to day what was going to happen next! I suppose that all of this was normal and proper for a child. But as I grew up, it became an escape mechanism and kept me from accomplishing the things I needed to do. And, too, I found it very easy to make up stories that exalted myself.

When as a young mother God began waking me every morning to converse with Him, He began to show me the dangers of my habit of daydreaming. With my busy family life I had no time for reading, but I could daydream as I worked. We scarcely had enough money for even necessities, so I imagined what I'd do with a million dollars if someone gave it to us. Since our family of six crowded our small house, I would imagine a large, beautiful home with a bedroom for each of the children. I would decorate it beautifully in my mind. Planning the yard in detail, I mentally planted it with flowers and bushes. I would imagine a lovely new car in the garage and new clothes for all our family. Such daydreams seemed harmless, and they brought me great pleasure and made me content with my lot in life.

But God said no. He wanted my mind free to hear His voice and think His thoughts. That was hard for me to accept. Even though His presence was very real and satisfied me fully, I was afraid to let go of the possibilities of my lifelong retreat. I delayed saying yes to God. Soon we moved to another town and church, and in the confusion I drifted back into daydreaming.

The extraordinary thing about this incident is that I *forgot*—yes, I *forgot*—that God had previously talked to me about this. I continued daydreaming through dull and unhappy times for many long years. It was not until the greatest sorrow of my life fell upon me that God, through sanctuary prayer, again spoke to me about the subject. At that time He reminded me that He had brought it to my attention before. The memory came flooding back.

This time I consciously made the decision to obey God and said, "Yes, Lord, I gladly give up daydreaming." What saddens me the most is looking back and realizing that God gave me the chance to walk with Him in special intimacy more than 30 years ago—and I turned it down! How much different my life would have been had I accepted His previous offer of help. How different would have been the lives of my children, my husband, the congregations we served. How much more able I would have been to witness for Him.

But God, in His kindness, did not abandon me, but pursued a different plan. Yes, He still spoke to me, guided me, and taught me. But that special intimacy was gone. It was 35 years before He could bring me around to face that same choice again!

My only solace in the face of my neglect is God's great comfort. He promises "a garment of praise" rather than a "spirit of despair" (Isa. 61:3). I praise God for His patience and love for me, for His willingness to accept me completely, for the opportunities to serve Him that He gives me today.

Others have experienced the same thing. A young man I

spoke with at a seminar I was attending told me a similar story. He said that recently God had brought to his attention something in his life that needed changing, and he suddenly remembered that God had spoken to him about the same thing 10 years before. But because he chose not to obey at that time, he had forgotten all about it for a decade.

But do not despair if this has also been your experience. God will not let you go. I remember the story of Abraham, who distrusted God's ability to save his life and so lied and said that his wife Sarah was his sister. He did it twice. We aren't told just how many years separated the two incidents, but finally God brought Abraham to the greatest test possible—surrendering his only son as a sacrifice to God. Praise the Lord, Abraham passed that test! But perhaps if he hadn't failed the other two times, God would not have found it necessary to bring him to the latter experience.

I'm thankful, though, for Abraham's story. And I'm glad God gave him that final test. It has comforted my heart so much and helped me to understand God's love for me.

And so I tell my story too. Oh, never say no to God. It will create in your life a great waste. Always respond to God when He speaks.

Over the years God has had a way of deliberately planting people in my life. Often I have felt that He gave them to me to pray for, love, and reach out to for special segments of time. A series of such experiences covered the four summers I worked toward a credential in library science. I was the librarian at one of our academies and spent the summers at one of our colleges. The first summer I spent two weeks attending a library workshop. My roommate was a Roman Catholic nun.

Sister Ann was more than 10 years older than I was and was librarian at a Catholic high school. From our very first encounter I felt God's presence in our relationship. It was the first time that Sister Ann had worn conventional clothing since she was 16 years old. Someone else had purchased the clothes she brought to the workshop, and she was awkward in them. I remember one very hot morning when she turned back after we had started for class, uncomfortable with having her arms exposed to public view for the first time in nearly 50 years! Returning to our room, she put on a sweater.

Sister Ann watched me closely in everything I did. I fixed our breakfasts in the little kitchen in the dorm and asked the blessing on our meals. For our worships, mornings and evenings, I read to her from a modern version of the New Testament that had just come out. We knelt in prayer together, and she used her rosary as I prayed.

She told me how she had joined the convent at 16, how concerned she was about the new nuns coming in, and about the many strange things that were happening since the nuns were allowed to wear street clothes. Some were wearing jewelry, and even smoking. I sensed in her a sincere devotion to God and truth. On the one Sabbath we were there together, Sister Ann went to church with me, telling me that her priest had suggested, "When in Rome, do as the Romans do." She was intensely interested in the Sabbath school lesson and the sermon. It was her first time in a Protestant church.

An announcement made in church said that Arthur White was going to be giving a slide presentation and talk about his grandmother, Ellen White, that afternoon at 3:00. I made a mental note that I would like to attend. Meanwhile friends invited me out to a picnic potluck. I invited Sister Ann to come along for the picnic, but she said that she had to do some studying, so I left her in our room.

As the hour for the program approached I became a little worried. I had to go back to the room to change my clothes but didn't want to ask Sister Ann to come along to the meeting with me. How could I explain Sister White to Sister Ann? Anyway, she was studying, I reasoned, and wouldn't want to come with me. I just won't mention it, I decided. But when I had changed my clothes I felt strongly impressed to invite her, and so I did, with trepidation. Eagerly she got up from her chair, exclaiming, "Oh, I hoped you would ask me to go!"

On the way to the program I briefly explained the prophetic work of Ellen White and her place in our church. Sister Ann was interested and remained so throughout the program. A few days before she left the campus at the end of the workshop, she visited the campus bookstore. Afterward she came back to the room to show me her purchases: a New Testament identical to mine, and copies of two books by Ellen White.

I kept in touch with Sister Ann for several years at Christmastime. But then she moved to a new convent, and I lost her address. I have often wondered what happened to this sweet woman that God placed in my life for those two weeks. As far as I understood I had obeyed God's directions in our relationship. But I have often wondered if in some way I could have been more aggressive in sharing my faith. Had fear, perhaps, stopped my ears to hearing God's voice?

The next summer I spent eight weeks at the same college. My roommate was the librarian of an academy in a neighboring conference. We had met before at curriculum meetings that our conferences shared and had arranged to room together. God gave us each other that summer as we studied together and prayed together for our children. It was a blessed summer, and Martha has been a friend ever since.

The third summer school session I roomed alone. But God planted another librarian in my life. Elsa, a public school elementary librarian, had no idea when she enrolled that she was attending a Seventh-day Adventist college—or even what Seventh-day Adventists were. She roomed three doors down from me in the basement of the girls' dorm. We had many of the same classes and so naturally gravitated toward each other, going to the dining hall together and studying together. I invited her to stop by my room every afternoon at 4:00 when she got out of a lab, and served her an iced fruit drink. Later she told me that it was just the time of day she always had a beer! God had directed me to fill her need. We studied together for tests, and I always prayed with her beforehand, asking God that we would go over the right things—and then again just before the tests— that we would remember what we had studied. We both did well in our classwork that summer.

Usually Elsa went home on the weekends, since she lived in a nearby city. But one weekend she stayed at college to get in some extra study. I explained that I did not study on the Sabbath hours, so she went over her notes alone. At sundown that Sabbath I distinctly felt God asking me to go down to her room and invite her to pray with me. Immediately I recoiled from that suggestion. What would Elsa think, anyway? I wondered. After all, she was busy studying.

But then I remembered hearing a seminar speaker say that when we are hesitant to obey God's voice about anything, we should ask ourselves, What is the worst thing that could happen to me if I do this?

So I asked myself, "What is the worst thing that could happen if I go down to Elsa's room to ask her to pray with me?"

"Well," I answered myself, "she could tell me she didn't want me to pray with her—that she was busy." I decided that I could handle that much rejection.

So I laughed to myself and said, "All right, Lord, I'll go."

I knocked on her door and she asked me in, seemingly glad to take a break in her studying.

"Elsa," I said, "I'm missing my husband. We usually pray together as the Sabbath closes, and I was wondering if you'd mind if I prayed with you, instead. We can pray for our children."

Elsa had confided to me earlier that her 16-year-old son was in trouble. She didn't like his friends, and she suspected that they were all using drugs. He had become extremely disrespectful to her, and her heart was aching.

So together Elsa and I knelt and I prayed for my children and for her son and his problems.

After prayer I went back to my room and got my books, and we spent the evening studying together.

The next morning the phone in my room rang at 7:30. It was an exuberant Elsa.

"Carrol," she exclaimed, "God answered your prayers. Last night at 11:30 my son called. He told me that he was sorry for causing me so much trouble, that he was straightening out his life. No more drugs. And he said he loved me." By that time both Elsa and I were crying. We praised the Lord together.

And I thought, *What if I hadn't gone to Elsa's room to pray?*

I was extremely glad that I had listened to God's voice.

The fourth summer school session God sent me another roommate—my college daughter, Julie. It greatly surprised me that she agreed to room with me. Since I was very busy with my studies and she worked in the biology department, we mostly went our own separate ways.

At the end of the summer she commented on the situation.

"You know, Mom, I had a lot of doubts about rooming with you."

I laughed. I'd had those doubts too.

"But you're the best roommate I've ever had," Julie concluded.

"Yes," I said, "I'm the *only* roommate you ever had who washed your clothes and made your bed!"

Yet I felt strongly that God had given Julie to me in a special way for those few short weeks of summer school—for whatever His reason.

It is important to put into practice immediately anything that God impresses us to do. As we obey, He will lead us further on. It reminds me of the lamp that a miner wears upon his hat. As he walks forward the light goes with him, but when he pauses the light stops too. We can see the path ahead spiritually only as we move forward in obedience.

God wants to be a living, daily presence in our lives. Responding to His voice makes that possible.

Summary

How we respond to God when He speaks to us determines how the relationship continues:

> Sometimes the response is praise,
> sometimes repentance from sin,
> sometimes action.

Putting into practice what God teaches me increases my ability to hear His voice.

Not responding will lessen my ability to recognize His words and sense His presence:

> Conviction fades.
> I am left in depression, darkness, or lukewarmness.

It deadens the conscience.

And it leads to bitterness, disillusionment, and wasted
　　years.

But God does not abandon us because of disobedience. He
will try again, as He did with Abraham.

When you are fearful of obeying God's voice, ask yourself:
What is the worst thing that could happen to me if I obey God
in this respect?

We will find that it's worth taking the risk of rejection.

It is important to put into practice immediately anything that
God impresses us to do.

As we obey, God will lead us further along.

God wants to be a living, daily presence in our lives.

Obedience to His voice makes that possible.

CHAPTER ELEVEN

The Inside Is Bigger Than the Outside

*M*y 9-year-old granddaughter, Tami, stood one morning before a mirror, her hands cupping her face as she turned her head this way and that, evaluating. "Isn't it amazing," she finally commented to her mother, who was working nearby, "how much bigger our heads are on the inside than they are on the outside?"

Tami's insight delighted me. How wonderful that a child should begin to comprehend the endless possibilities of the power and scope of the human mind. God's inward voice operates even in the mind of a child!

Learning to listen to His voice is possible only because of the human mind. How beautifully God designed it! King David said:

"I praise you because I am fearfully
  and wonderfully made;
  your works are wonderful,
  I know that full well" (Ps. 139:14).

It is only through the mind that God can reach a human soul. Prayer, the two-way communication between earth and heaven, works through the mind. The five senses—taste, touch, smell, hearing, and sight—are the avenues through which either good or evil enters. Our responses to what reaches our minds through these avenues will either sharpen our spiritual hearing or deaden it.

If the mind were really as small as the head, how easy it would be to control it. But no, as Tami noted, the inside is much, much larger than the outside! You see, our minds contain the record of our lifetime, most of it stored away in the unconscious where we seldom give it any thought at all. Yet we are told that the unconscious mind determines around 80 percent of the way we respond to life's experiences. We react the way we do because of what has happened to us in the past. And we aren't even conscious of it!

When I accepted Jesus as my Saviour and yielded the control center of my mind to God, I had no idea of all the garbage stored away in my unconscious, some of it inherited and some of it cultivated. Or that Satan had cleverly learned to bypass our mental control centers to tempt even Christians into sin. But, praise the Lord, one of the important jobs of the Holy Spirit is to reveal to us bit by bit what lies buried in our subconscious. As we ask forgiveness for the sins of the past and turn them over to God for cleansing, we are able to intelligently counter Satan's attempts to plug directly into the unconscious mind. Then we can clearly hear the voice of God saying, "This is the way; walk in it" (Isa. 30:21).

Why doesn't God just clean out the whole mess at once and be done with it? That's a question I used to ask. But you see, God values our freedom so much that He won't do that. He wants us to see the depths of our need of Him, to comprehend our sinfulness, and to cooperate with Him in the cleansing. After all, He made us in His image. He wants us to work alongside Him in the rebuilding of our lives and the cleansing of our minds. Every change in our lives is to be done in concert with Jesus, the Holy Spirit, and the angels. This combined union will build strong characters.

Always keep in mind that God is not a magician. We're used to magic in today's world—and I'm not talking here about sleight-of-hand tricks. No, the supernatural is present in many current television shows, books, etc. Magic appeals to the human nature. It's so easy. Even Christians often unconsciously choose magic over miracles because we feel no need to comprehend magic, but it unsettles us not to be able to understand miracles. Magic makes no demands of us. Presto, it's done! We need sacrifice nothing. What we don't realize is that while miracles are real, magic is only a delusion. But God never deals in magic. It is Satan's counterfeit for God's miracles.

I'm speaking firsthand about this subject, for God has shown me how interspersed with my spiritual concepts has been belief in spiritual magic—the expectation of something for nothing— great gain, no pain.

I have always been a lover of stories—adventure, courage, love, magic. Of course, I knew that magic was impossible—not real. But when I read of the miracles of Jesus I unconsciously combined the counterfeit with the true. Christians must be careful not to absorb the world's belief in magic and just apply it to God. The Lord works in a totally different way. Magic is fake, while miracles are real. Moses performed miracles before the pharaoh of Egypt. Pharaoh's wise men worked magic that closely resembled what Moses had done. But while magic eventually evaporates, miracles last forever.

The miracle that God wants to work in our lives is the complete rebuilding of our characters. Magic holds no lasting happiness for anyone, but the miracle of a holy character will give us eternal happiness. Miracles are God's initiative, not ours. A miracle will always change us so that our life will never be quite the same again. And a miracle never backfires. Ten years from now I will still realize that the miracle God worked in my life today was exactly what I needed.

The Bible calls such daily miracles the process of sanctification. It is day-by-day growth. By it God prepares us to live in heaven with the angels. The gradual rebuilding of our minds and lives is as truly a miracle as is the instant miracle of new birth. When Jesus turned the water into wine at the wedding feast in Cana, He only accelerated the process by which all food comes into being. It was the very same miracle of life that we take part in every day. All food is a miracle from God, though He allows the sun and rain, the nutrients in the soil, and even our human hands to take part—to be instruments—in union with Him in producing our food. Just so in renewing our minds God has slowed down the miracle so that we can intelligently cooperate with Him in the perfecting of our minds and bodies. He wants us to be comfortable in the companionship of holy beings. Because God created us in His image, He knows that even here on earth our minds can stretch and grow and comprehend ideas that are right now incomprehensible to us.

God's most effective tools for digging down into our unconscious minds are trials, sorrow, grief, and pain. Oh, we don't like those! But I can tell you that the joy outweighs the pain. And it is in submitting to God's refining that we will find true happiness.

Here is yet another way to cultivate hearing God's voice: *choose today to cooperate with God in the renewal of your mind.* Give Him permission to remove the rubbish from your unconscious mind so that you no longer live in the past but by your conscious choice in the present.

When I made this choice I had no idea what I was beginning. But I have never regretted it for a moment. Actually, it's a lot like going backpacking. If I had known the pain involved with backpacking before I went on my first trip, I would never have gone. But the joy and exhilaration of mountains, the wildflowers, the rivers, the blue sky, the starry nights—all these outweighed the pain. It's the same with our expedition with God. If you look only at the pain, it isn't worth it. But when you experience the joy, the *companionship of Jesus*—why, the pain is hardly worth mentioning.

You'd never think that the mind, housed completely within your brain, which in turn is confined within the bones and skin of one small head, could contain enough space to explore for an entire lifetime. But it does. And it's an exciting journey.

I consciously began this journey when I began practicing sanctuary prayer. As I followed the sanctuary steps in my daily prayer time (listed in chapter 3), I discovered that God had radical plans for reconverting me. It was both exciting and frightening. I kept expecting Him to be finished. But I now know that my expedition with God will not end until Jesus comes again—

and in heaven we will begin an eternal spiritual trek.

For a long time I used to worry because I didn't know what sins God had recorded about me on the books of heaven. How could I know that I had confessed each one? What a relief it has been as I have studied the sanctuary to realize that Jesus, my high priest, has set aside a special place—the Most Holy Place of the sanctuary in heaven—and a special time—the day of investigative judgment—to reveal to me exactly what the books of heaven contain on me. He is hiding nothing. All that limits the completion of this task is my human inability to accept immediately His words as true. It takes time for me to see the seriousness of God's disclosures. But God is willing to give each of us the time that we need.

Not long ago God surprised me with a strange little series of circumstances. They began on one of the first really hot days of summer—the first day, in fact, that we had turned on our air conditioner for the season. At our house we had a habit of switching off the air conditioner about 6:00 or 7:00 in the evening, as soon as the air outside began to cool down. Then we would open up all the windows for the night and close them again in the morning, waiting until nearly noon to turn on the air conditioner.

This particular night we had turned off the air conditioner, and the windows were wide open when I went to bed. It was still warm, and I drifted off to sleep lying on top of the covers. Soon, though, I awakened to discover that the breeze blowing in the window over my bed was quite chilly and I was cold. So I got under the covers and cuddled down to sleep again.

But before long I was awake, this time perspiring in the heat. Once more I threw off the covers and fell asleep. The annoying part of the experience was that it kept recurring all night long. Heat, cold, heat, cold, heat. I spent a most restless night.

Toward morning I got up to go to the bathroom. As I passed the air vent I realized that the heater was on! No wonder I was restless. Because the heater switch had been flipped, the cold air from the window that chilled me also caused the thermostat to turn the heater on, which in turn caused me to start perspiring.

As the heater warmed the house the thermostat shut off the heater, and once again the cool breeze chilled me. Over and over all night.

Immediately I went out into the hall, shut off the heater, and returned to bed. It was obvious that whoever had turned off the air conditioner the night before had inadvertently flipped the switch completely to the right to "heat" instead of leaving it in the center at "off."

In the morning I disgustedly confronted my husband. "Do you know what you did last night? When you turned off the air conditioner you turned on the heat!" Then I related the experience to him. A sound sleeper, he had slept comfortably through the night.

"Well, I surely don't remember doing that!" my husband exclaimed.

"Of course you don't," I said. "You didn't do it on purpose."

We dropped the subject, and neither of us mentioned it again. Later that day, however, when we were verbalizing on some other subject entirely, I heard my husband mutter a little aside that made no sense to me at the time but that I somehow stored away in a corner of my mind to think about later. What he said was, "I get blamed for a lot of things around here that I don't do." Somehow God impressed me that his remark would have some future meaning for me. But I did not deal with it at that time.

Several days later I went into my bathroom and noticed my washcloth hung up wrong side out. Now, I like a neat house, and I have spent years training my family to hang up towels and washcloths properly. As my eye fell on my wash cloth my immediate reaction was "Now what has John been doing with my washcloth?" But just as immediately I realized how ridiculous my response was. It was plain to me that I myself had inadvertently hung the cloth up wrong side out. Just then God spoke to me in my thoughts: "And *you* turned on the heat!" In amazement I realized that it was most likely so. I am the one who usually turns off the air conditioner and opens the windows at night. No doubt I was the one who had done so that night.

Then why was it that without any question at all I immediately blamed my husband? His plaintive remark of a few days before came clearly into my mind: "I get blamed for a lot of things around here that I don't do."

I humbled myself before the Lord. It was obvious to me that something important was taking place.

"Just what are You trying to tell me, Lord?" I questioned. God went on to reveal to me that my habit of blaming others for my own carelessness had been a lifelong escape mechanism of mine. By it I could avoid being in the wrong. Shaking my head in amazement, I began to realize how much distress I had caused my husband over the years. And doubtless my children as well.

"Lord," I prayed, "I ask Your forgiveness. I need to be changed. Blot out my sin, I pray, and change me into Your likeness. May I willingly and intelligently take the blame for my own mistakes."

Later that same day God reinforced my need of change. As I went out into the living room about noon I found the sliding glass door still open although the air conditioner was already on. My first thought was *Now why did John leave that door open?* Immediately I had to laugh, for he had been gone since early morning, and it was my responsibility anyway.

"I'm hopeless, Lord," I confessed. "Please change me."

Of course, I knew I had to confess to my husband as well as to God. That evening I told him the complete story of how God had revealed to me my problem in this area. I asked John to forgive me for the sadness I had caused him over the years. And do you know what my husband did? He came over to me and put his arms around me and said, "You don't need to ask my forgiveness. There is nothing to forgive. You have always been a good wife to me."

"Yes," I told him, "I need to ask your forgiveness for my own sake and for God's. Your love for me may have hidden this sin from you, but I still know that it made your life a little heavier because you have had to carry blame that was not yours. I want to be a different sort of wife to you from now on. I want to carry the blame for my own mistakes and leave you free."

God is interested in Christian development first of all in the home. And no matter how old we are, He can do the impossible—change our character and habits. That is the business of the investigative judgment as God prepares a people to translate at His coming.

The Lord has great plans for the consecrated human mind even here on earth. He wants to cleanse it of sin, empty it of nonessentials, and fill and enlarge it with His thoughts, His plans. My granddaughter Tami was right when she noted that the inside of the head is so much larger than the outside. By giving us His own great thoughts, God desires to stretch our minds permanently so that He can give us more and more of Himself.

Summary

It is only through the mind that God can reach a human soul.

Prayer, the two-way communication between earth and heaven, works through the mind. The five senses—taste, touch, smell, hearing, and sight—permit either good or evil to enter. Our response to them will either sharpen or deaden our spiritual hearing.

The human mind contains the record of our lifetime, most of it stored away in the unconscious.

The unconscious mind determines around 80 percent of the way we respond to life's experiences. We react the way we do today because of what happened to us in our yesterdays. And we aren't even aware of it.

One of the important jobs of the Holy Spirit is to reveal to us bit by bit what lies buried in our subconscious so that we can ask forgiveness and turn it all over to Him for cleansing.

God is not a magician. He does not just whisk away all the secrets of our past. Magic is Satan's counterfeit for God's miracles. Miracles last, while magic is delusionary.

The Lord works two miracles in the born-again Christian's life: one, the instant miracle of justification—or conversion—in which we give God the control center of our mind. Two, He performs the day-by-day growth of sanctification in which God renews even our subconscious minds. Every change in our lives must come as a result of our own choice in concert with Jesus, the Holy Spirit, and the angels.

Because God has made us in His image, He wants us to have an active part in such transformation. He knows that even here on earth our minds can stretch and grow to think His thoughts.

Choose today to cooperate with God in the renewing of your mind.

Jesus, our High Priest, has set aside a special place (the Most Holy Place of the heavenly sanctuary) and a special time (the day of investigative judgment) to reveal to us what heaven has recorded about us. It is His desire to uncover the secrets that we have hidden even from ourselves so that the Holy Spirit can completely *renew* our minds.

By giving us His own great thoughts, God desires to stretch our minds permanently so that He can give us more and more of Himself.

CHAPTER TWELVE

Healing the Broken

The mind stores memories safely away in various files, tagged with unconscious keys. Every now and then something in the present will bring up from the unconscious mind a series of memories with similar tags.

Because God was the one who designed the mind to work like it does, we can expect that He made it that way for a purpose. It is His plan to use such recalled memories to aid in the renewing of our minds. As one by one God brings past experiences into our consciousness, He desires that we repent of sin connected with them and learn the lessons they can teach us. God is preparing a people for whom memory can hold no surprises and no fear. While He uses only truth in His management of the mind, Satan is free to employ delusion. How important, then, that the mind always be under divine control.

Jeremiah describes the human mind:

"The heart is deceitful above all things
and beyond cure.
Who can understand it?
I the Lord search the heart
and examine the mind,
to reward a man according to his conduct,
according to what his deeds deserve" (Jer. 17:9, 10).

But the prophet added his confidence in God's ability to heal even the diseased mind:

"Heal me, O Lord, and I will be healed;
  save me and I will be saved,
  for you are the one I praise" (verse 14).

As God's people cooperate with Him in confessing their past sins, Satan will no longer be able to tempt them into present sin by throwing up the past in their faces. They will understand their weaknesses and be able to thwart Satan in his attempts to control them through the stored memories in the unconscious mind.

God desires an intelligent people, unencumbered with baggage, either real or imagined, from the past. When we begin to understand the work that God is doing in our minds and lives we can grasp more fully why it is extremely important that we cooperate with Him in keeping the lines of communication open between earth and heaven. He wants to take our weak, sinful human minds, defective as they are, and heal them so that we can assimilate the secrets of His kingdom.

I was 14 the Christmas my little sister did her Christmas shopping for the first time with money she had earned herself. Her gift to me was an adorable ceramic donkey, six and one-half inches tall, a little less in length, creamy tan in color with brown hooves, tail tip, mane, eyes, and assorted spots and with pink-lined ears and nostrils. Loving him the minute I unwrapped him, I christened him Bimbo.

Opal's gift to my older sister was a matching deer, blue in color, that Ardith called Bambi. We set the two little figures up on the table side by side and looked them over with delight. Because we dearly loved our little sister, those first gifts of hers were precious to us. She had chosen them herself and paid for them (25 cents each) with money she had earned herself. Bimbo and Bambi were our favorite gifts that Christmas.

Bimbo accompanied me to boarding school and not only made a dormitory room seem like home but furnished art inspiration for a school notebook. I drew Bimbo facing forward on the front cover, turned tail on the back.

When I married, Bimbo helped me feel at home immediately in my new surroundings. My young husband, John, found the perfect spot for Bimbo's display in our new home—the bottom shelf of an intricate Chippendale-style hanging cabinet that he had made himself in woodworking class in college. Thus our two pasts joined to decorate our home together.

Because John was a young minister, we moved often those first few years. Carefully I packed Bimbo each time we moved, and as I unpacked I set him once again in his special place on the Chippendale shelf.

When our second son was born my husband brought me home from the hospital with eagerness. He loved to surprise me, and in my absence he had wallpapered the dining room in our little house and bought new window blinds and white ruffled curtains for the two windows, plus new sheer curtains for the living room—all things that homemaker me had been openly yearning for. I rejoiced in the picture book look of my new home, the reunion with my 18-month-old son, and the presence of our new baby. I felt so loved!

Then a few days later I was sitting in the living room admiring the new beauty of my home when my glance swept the Chippendale shelf. Instantly I looked again. No Bimbo. Quickly my eyes roamed the room. Perhaps John had put the figurine elsewhere in the newly decorated room. But I could not see him anywhere. To say that I was disturbed is putting it mildly.

"John," I called in agitation, "where is Bimbo?"

His downcast face shocked me.

"You—you didn't *break* him, did you?" I exclaimed in horror.

Crossing the room to the Chippendale shelf, he opened the small drawer at the bottom. There—in pieces—was my little donkey.

My face became hard.

"Just throw him away," I said in a cold voice.

"I think I can glue him together so you'll hardly notice," he said as he fitted the pieces together in his hands.

"No," I said, "he'd still be broken. I don't want him anymore.

Just throw him away."

"I'm so sorry, dear," John said. "I know he meant a lot to you."

Taking the pieces of ceramic, he found a good glue and reconstructed the jaunty donkey and set him once more upon the Chippendale shelf. But in my mind he was no longer my sweet donkey. He was broken. I never smiled upon him again and only tolerated his presence in my home because I realized that John wanted so much to atone for breaking my little treasure.

Bimbo moved again and again with our growing family. We changed his special place from the Chippendale shelf to the top of the small piano that added music to our home. From the piano top he eyed four budding musicians as they practiced piano, trumpet, and clarinet.

My husband wrote a lilting little song for the children's amusement:

> Bimbo, the spotted donkey,
> What have you got to say?
> Bimbo, the spotted donkey,
> Where have you been today?
>
> I've been out to play,
> I've been eating hay,
> Bimbo, the spotted donkey,
> That's what he has to say.

And so for many years my broken donkey was a part of our lives. But not of my heart. I handled him carelessly, willing him to break again so that I could throw him away.

And one day it happened. Unpacking in a new home, I found the figurine in pieces.

"I think I can fix him again," John anxiously volunteered, examining the pieces.

"No way! This time we throw that donkey away!" I exclaimed. "You know I don't like broken things." I dumped the pieces unceremoniously into the trash.

Somewhere along my spiritual journey, soon after I began sanctuary prayer, I began to be uncomfortable with my dislike of broken things. But it is only lately that God opened up to me that it is a major character flaw—an outward sign of my inward exactitude, my impatience with less than perfection not only in things but also in people.

You see, God loves broken things with a more special love than He loves perfect, unflawed things. The Bible tells us this. Jesus Himself was *broken* so that He could save all broken people. It's true that the glue that God uses to repair people is better than that which John employed to put Bimbo back together with, but still the repair work is plainly visible in most of us. We present flawed surfaces to the rest of the world and the universe, and it will be that way until we enter eternity. Do we love each other in spite of our flaws? Can we love broken things? Can we possibly love each other *because* of the brokenness?

I was walking the aisles of the swap meet the other Sunday and stopped abruptly at one display. There, amid other junk and trivia, stood a small ceramic donkey with brown spots and pink ears—a twin to the long-ago discarded Bimbo.

"How much?" I asked the seller as I examined the figurine carefully. (I almost expected him to be repaired in just the same places as Bimbo had been—but he had no fracture lines. His only imperfection was that age had worn away some of the brown on his mane and hooves.)

"A dollar and a half," the man answered, adding the time-worn refrain of the swap meet, "He's old, I think."

Pulling out my dollar and two quarters, I paid the man. Carefully I watched over the wrapping—two paper bags to cushion my little donkey—and carried him away.

"Look," I wanted to say to the vendor, "he's not so very old. He was *new* when I was 14. And he cost only 25 cents brand-new!"

Once again Bimbo decorates my living room. This time he shares a shelf in a bookcase with several books and a doll. He is a continual reminder to me of my brokenness before God and of God's mending abilities and *love* for broken things.

My "happy ever after" mentality would wish that I had learned my lesson from this one experience and could now deal graciously—and lovingly—with broken things and broken people. But it's not true, of course. Most of God's miracles in my life consist of *growth,* not instant change. The Lord had more to show me on the same subject. He pulled another memory out of my past.

The last few weeks before our first child was born I had a doctor's appointment every Thursday afternoon. Carrie, a girl whom I had known slightly from college days, also had a Thursday afternoon appointment with the same doctor and was also expecting her first child. So week by week we two mothers-to-be eagerly discussed the long-awaited arrivals. We made arrangements to get together with our babies after their birth.

One Thursday, just days before our babies were due to be born, when I arrived for my appointment I noticed that Carrie was obviously uncomfortable.

"I think I'm in labor," she said. *Lucky girl,* I thought, wishing it were me. Sure enough, the doctor verified that she was ready to deliver, and she departed for the hospital. And I went home to wait.

The next day I called her home to find out what she had had. But her baby had been born dead.

The news devastated me. I began to have visions of my baby being born dead, too. All ungrounded, of course. I gave birth three weeks later to a healthy ten-and-a-half-pound son.

As I admired my perfect little boy I remembered Carrie's and my excited plans to get together with our children. Somehow I persuaded myself that she would want to see my baby even though she had lost hers. In my immaturity I did not recognize the issue from her side at all—only my own selfish desire to show off my beautiful baby. So I went to see her. I will say that she was kinder than I was. She treated me politely, though not warmly, and admired my son. A little uneasy about the whole thing, I left quickly and put the affair out of my mind.

Until last week, that is.

As I was housecleaning, the whole story came back in every

uneasy detail.

"Oh, no," I shuddered, "how could I have ever been so thoughtless? I'm surely glad that I am more mature now."

And again I put the incident out of my mind.

The next morning as I was at the altar of sacrifice in my sanctuary prayer time, my experience of showing off my live baby to the mother whose infant had died flashed into my mind with heartrending clarity. It dawned on me that God was bringing the incident into my consciousness for a purpose. Immediately I confessed my sin of thoughtlessness in causing needless pain to Carrie, and asked God's forgiveness for my past sin.

There, I had taken care of that. I laid the uncomfortable memory to rest again.

Several days later I was sitting on the couch in the living room editing this chapter on broken things. I had read only the first two paragraphs when the whole scene of me with my live baby, Carrie with her sorrow, flashed into my mind again with great pain—as though I were the one who had lost the baby. This time I was bewildered.

"God," I said, "I asked You to forgive any sin connected with this part of my past. I took care of all that the other day. Now why is it bothering me again? It is all in the past."

"No," He clearly said, "it is not all in the past. It's in the present."

By this time I really felt disturbed. Getting up from the couch, I went out to the kitchen—as though I could escape the voice of God. As I stood in the middle of the kitchen, I asked, "What do You mean, it's in the present? I don't understand."

"You're still the same," God explained. "You eagerly bound up to people to share all the exciting things you are involved in, while often they have just buried all their hopes and dreams. It's right now that this is happening, not in the past."

Then God brought to my mind a recent encounter with a woman who had lost all hope in life. Because I didn't know how to relate to her sorrow and pain, I had babbled on about myself. Yes, it was true. I was still showing off my live baby to people who had lost theirs.

Oh, Lord, forgive me. Create in me the ability to view life through the eyes and hearts of others. Teach me how to bring hope, encouragement, and joy to those who have lost their dreams. And cultivate in me the ability to clearly hear Your voice and cooperate with You in the retraining of my mind.

I'm so glad that God loves broken things. I still need mending. And, praise God, He's still in the business of gluing me back together.

Summary

God is daily recalling to our consciousness stored memories from our unconscious to aid in the renewing of our minds.

As we repent of any sin in connection with these recalled memories, God is able to blot out our sin from His records in heaven and cleanse our memories of sin and heartache.

Thus Satan is blocked in his familiar tactic of seeking to control our thoughts and actions through plugging directly into our unconscious minds and bypassing the control center where we can make intelligent choices.

God desires an intelligent people, unencumbered with emotional baggage from the past, and wholly able to *reason* out immediate responses to every life situation.

The Lord loves broken things. It is His plan to take repaired human beings and place them nearest His throne throughout eternity. Jesus Himself became broken for us.

He desires for us to cultivate that same love for other broken human beings around us.

CHAPTER THIRTEEN

What Shall I Do With My Pride?

*T*here once was a lady
      (I won't admit it was me)
Who longed and who dreamed
      of the great work she'd do—
      the books she'd write
          everyone would praise,
          the lectures she'd give—
          why, demand for her talks
          would spread north and south,
             east and west.
      Hardly anyone
          anywhere
      but would know her name.
Of course, this dream was all for the Lord,
Oh yes, she wanted to witness for God.
      Only God—oh my, she desired
      only to be His instrument, yes!

One day as she dreamed, she read
      from the Book
      God's words
and He plainly said,
      "Should you then seek great things
      for yourself?
      Seek them not" (Jer. 45:5).

She stopped short, amazed.
Yes, God had spoken, and her dreams
            of acclaim must be cast away.

"Enter through the narrow gate," Christ said.
"For wide is the gate and broad is the road
that leads to destruction, and many
            enter through it.
But small is the gate and narrow the road
that leads to life, and only a few
            find it" (Matt. 7:13, 14).

Whenever this lady
            (I still won't admit it is me)
is tempted to pleasure herself
            with dreams of acclaim,
a clear voice reminds,
            "Should you seek great things
            for yourself?
            Seek them not."
And she turns to the narrow road
and joyfully travels on,
for Jesus walks there
and the destination gleams
ahead like a shining star.
(Oh, yes, of course, the lady *is* me!)

Well, there you have it. You can see that God has been having a busy time dealing with me! I'm glad that He has all the time He needs to deal with each of us. He is eager to draw ever closer to us in the intimate family relationship He desires with every member of humanity. Each of us has battles to fight with self. Pride has been one of my toughest. Along, of course, with the rest of pride's relatives: resentment, self-pity, jealousy, complaining, indolence, worry, anger, and low self-esteem.

I discovered the verse I have quoted to begin this chapter in an old poetry scrapbook of mine. I wrote it in 1983, not know-ing, of course, that I really would write books and give talks! But God was preparing me then to yield to Him my pride.

What shall I do with my pride? As pointed out to me by the inward voice of the Holy Spirit, I can do only one thing with it—confess it and give it to Jesus and ask Him to rid me of this worst-of-all sin.

It has often seemed to me that if I were proud of something that I had done that was really praiseworthy, well, perhaps, that would be excusable. But so far, I see that my pride, like my fear, is usually completely unreasonable in nature. Even in my state of pride I can recognize that I really have nothing to be proud of! And how Satan must laugh as he pulls his little strings and pushes his little buttons to make me proud.

But—praise the Lord—God is giving me victory! He is daily at work in my life to uncover the roots of this sin and lay it bare. And I am daily yielding my all to Him and cooperating with Him in this painful task.

I was still in grade school when I recognized the unreason-ableness of my pride. For example, I remember that as our class sang hymns together I began to sing loudly. Shortly I began to hope that the rest of the children would hear me. I felt proud of my singing. But at the same time I knew that I really was not mu-sically gifted and did not have a good voice. The paradox of my thoughts puzzled me. As I walked home from school I wondered what in the world was going on in my mind that I should feel such unreasonable pride in the face of reality.

Not all of my readers battle the same sort of pride I en-counter. But you battle something. Pride has many faces. It keeps me from being warm and friendly to those who seem cold to me. Or it prevents me from reaching out to others for fear of rejection. Pride hides the needs of others from me as I center in on my own. It makes me cater to socially important people and ignore the lonely and needy. Pride is always attractive to the nat-ural human heart.

When I began practicing sanctuary prayer and daily knelt at the altar of sacrifice—confessing my sinful acts and tenden-

cies—and began consciously cooperating with Jesus in the retraining of my mind, I felt sure that I had seen the last of pride.
Surely pride would be the first thing eliminated from my life, I
thought, because I realized how greatly God disliked it. I recalled His scathing denunciation of the proud priests and
Pharisees of His day. Surely He feels the same today.

But pride, instead of being the first sin to go, is the last.
Satan's basic sin, it is ingrained into the very depths of each of
us. We must learn to loathe any sign of pride in ourselves and to
immediately yield it up to Jesus. (I am not speaking of the positive side of pride, such as delight in doing a job well, pleasure
in looking attractive, or joy in creative abilities. They are the re-
wards that joy in life brings about. In my denunciation of pride
I am speaking only of *unreasonable* pride obsessed with self and
that enslaves and hinders us from being useful in God's kingdom.)

Two young men, members of the church where my husband
pastored, entered the ministry in a distant conference. When
one of the young men came back to our church after his first in-
terview with the president of the other conference, he gave a report in our church of what had happened.

"The president is a very godly man," our friend said, "and I
was especially impressed with his wife. An unusual president's
wife, she leads inner-city ministries and is a praying woman. She
reminds me of our pastor's wife."

That was all he said. At least that is all I heard. I felt the faint
stirring of pride. So this wonderful president's wife was like
me—well! But I recognized pride and gave it a swift kick, and it
retreated. Then I forgot all about the incident—or did I?

Several months later a young couple who had visited our
two young friends in their faraway conference visited our
church to show slides they had taken while there and report on
the progress of the two men. The man gave the Sabbath school
talk and spoke often of the wonderful president's wife and her
missionary zeal and accomplishments. Inside I felt a nudge.
"That's the woman who is so much like you, isn't it?" a voice
asked. I aimed another kick at pride, and it quieted down again.

After church, as I was leaving to go to my car, I met the young wife of the man who had presented the Sabbath school report.

"You know," she said, "you remind me so much of that conference president's wife! When you were greeting the people this morning in church and asking for prayer requests, you sounded just like her. Both of you have the same warm way of reaching out to people." I thanked her and got into my car to wait for my husband. Pride was having a heyday in my mind. And my kicks didn't seem to quiet it down a bit. I prayed all the way home from church, but the battle continued.

I struggled through Sabbath afternoon, Sunday, and into Monday, trying to keep my mind full of useful thoughts, dreading the times that pride would begin its harangues about how great I was. Finally, on Monday afternoon I told my husband about my problem.

"I was sure," I said to him, "that I could handle this through prayer. I resist the thoughts every time they come. But it is a constant battle. I can't let up for a second. I am so tired. Will you pray for me?"

We knelt by the living room couch, and my husband asked God to rebuke Satan in the name of Jesus. Immediately I sensed freedom. The name of Jesus has power.

I don't know why my prayers alone did not rid me of this attack. For some reason this time I needed my husband's prayers. I remembered that Jesus told His disciples on one occasion: "Again, I tell you that if two of you on earth agree about anything you ask for, it will be done for you by my Father in heaven. For where two or three come together in my name, there am I with them" (Matt. 18:19, 20).

Praying together with someone else brings added power. I have learned to never hesitate to enlist the prayers of others on my behalf.

Sometimes pride comes in from another angle.

One Sabbath afternoon I was sitting in my living room remembering the morning church service. A young woman had given a talk and done quite well. She had good stage presence and a good message. But every now and then something she said or did was quite awkward, and I felt that it spoiled her presentation. As I was contemplating her awkwardness, the Lord spoke to me, "She is just like you."

"Do You mean, Lord, that I am awkward in public speaking?" I asked in surprise.

"Yes, you are," He answered.

"Well, Lord," I said, "if I'm awkward in public speaking, I just won't give any more talks. That's all right with me. I'll just spend my time in writing. I wouldn't want to dishonor You by my awkwardness."

"No," the Lord remonstrated, "pride is speaking through you right now. I want you to continue speaking in public, but always remember that of yourself you are awkward. Your strength and power in speaking come only from Me. Without Me you can do nothing."

Since that encounter I have contemplated what God was trying to tell me. One thing I have noticed is that some of the most effective Christian speakers are not particularly smooth and polished speakers. Yet their sincerity and honesty reach out and touch hearts. They are approachable, and their listeners can identify readily with them.

Of course, it would never do for me to use that fact as an excuse for not improving my own public-speaking abilities. I believe that God wants us to enhance our effectiveness in witnessing and to do our very best. But I always remember that without God I can do nothing. And this protects me from pride.

Just after Thanksgiving this past year I was musing on how the Lord has been leading me. I reflected on how He is using me to reach many people not only through my books, but also through speaking. I had just completed two seminars in which He had especially blessed, and I had felt great freedom in speaking. It greatly pleased me that He could use me.

God's voice interrupted my musing.

"I could even use a rock," He said.

Instantly I remembered the story of the triumphal entry of Jesus into Jerusalem just before His death. As the people shouted praises and hosannas to Jesus, the Pharisees asked Him to rebuke His disciples.

"I tell you," He replied, "if they keep quiet, the stones will cry out" (Luke 19:40).

Humbled, I thanked the Lord for showing up my human pride. And for allowing me to be a stone in His kingdom.

What shall I do with my pride? There is only one thing I can do with pride as God reveals it to me through the inward voice of the Holy Spirit. Confess it as sin, and allow God to purge me from even its residue. I thank Jesus, my high priest, that it is His work during this day of atonement to completely cleanse me of pride.

Summary

Pride is the greatest foe we face in our judgment journey. Its relatives include resentment, self-pity, jealousy, complaining, indolence, worry, anger, and low self-esteem.

The nature of the beast is its unreasonableness. Even though with our intellect we recognize the illogic of our pride, yet with our emotions it still tempts.

Pride hinders my Christian walk by keeping me from being friendly to those who seem cold to me and from reaching out to others for fear of rejection. As I center in on my own needs it prevents me from seeing those of others. It makes me cater to socially important people and ignore the lonely and needy. Pride is always attractive to the natural human heart.

The last sin to be totally defeated in the human heart, pride was Lucifer's original sin, and it lies ingrained in the depths of each of us.

What shall I do with my pride? Confess it as sin, and allow God to purge every trait of it from me. That is the business of the investigative judgment.

CHAPTER 14

Shutting Off and Turning On

*I*t is God's plan that as we interrelate with Him and cultivate hearing His voice we become more and more intelligent about how to control our minds. In order to keep that control, I need to shut off as many of the voices of the world as possible, either that of my own carnal nature or those of the godless world. Therefore as I block off the world's voices, I must turn on the voice of God to fill my mind.

In *Practical Pointers to Personal Prayer* I tell a story that I will briefly relate again. I described how one time I stood at the kitchen sink feeling sorry for myself as I did the dishes while others in the family were having a good time in the living room. As I was wallowing in self-pity I heard God speak to me.

"You don't have to think these thoughts," He said.

The idea startled me.

"Wha-at?" I stammered.

"You don't have to think these thoughts," He repeated.

And I realized that it was true. I was indulging myself in self-pity, deliberately prolonging the exquisite agony of self-destructive thoughts. But God had given me the control of my mind. I didn't have to dwell on such things. Instead I could choose to shut them out and deliberately focus on pleasant thoughts.

Abandoning my self-pity, I praised God instead. That encounter with God through His inward voice has changed my life. Often when I am tempted by Satan to indulge in self-pity, as I did so often in the past, I hear God's inward voice again: "You don't have to think those thoughts." And I immediately use my power of choice to change the tenor of my thoughts from self-pity, resentment, anger, or pride, to constructive things.

My inner thoughts are easier to handle if I have shut out the more vocal voices of the world. Perhaps it might mean different things to different people. It's obvious to all of us that movies of violence and sex are worldly voices. But many television programs are just as blatant. I know I cannot listen to the radio and television all day or read secular magazines and books, and then expect to immediately change to spiritual thoughts in my worship time. The average person represented in magazines and on television has no thought of God, worships only human wisdom, and is obsessed with self. The viewer or listener easily and subtly absorbs such premises. So I limit myself even in watching the news and other seemingly harmless programs, always ending my day with Bible study, contemplation, and prayer. If we are to live the life of Enoch, we must be watchful. Satan's voices are exceedingly loud, and many of them are attractive and alluring.

Worldly voices fill even shopping malls. Rock music, carnal pictures, materialism—all shout out the sentiments of the world. I often come home from a shopping expedition with no attraction for spiritual things. But if I immediately seek a quiet spot to read a Bible passage I am refreshed and rejuvenated, once again clearly hearing God's voice. I have shut out the world and turned my mind toward Jesus.

Sometimes it is necessary to spend time in the world. Many Christians spend a good part of every day at work in non-Christian environments. When that is necessary, God is able to give them a hiding place inside their minds to commune with Him in the midst of confusion and worldliness. Those who work in such places have shared with me their unique ways of tuning out the world and turning on the voice of God. They read a scripture on morning and noon breaks and look for opportunities to witness to their fellow employees. The same God who is willing and able to awaken us each morning to study and pray is just as eager to show us how to commune with Him throughout the day. In fact, if we have spent that quality time with God in the early-morning hours before work, we can *know* that He will send His presence with us throughout the day.

"Amid the hurrying throng, and the strain of life's intense activities, he who is thus refreshed [by spending time with Jesus in the morning] will be surrounded with an atmosphere of light and peace. He will receive a new endowment of both physical and mental strength. His life will breathe out a fragrance, and will reveal a divine power that will reach men's hearts" *(The Ministry of Healing,* p. 58).

Here is good advice from David, the great king of Israel, on how to turn off the voices of the world and hear that of God:

"Blessed is the man [or woman]
   who does not walk in the counsel
      of the wicked
   or stand in the way of sinners
   or sit in the seat of mockers.
But his delight is in the law of the Lord,
   and on his law he meditates day and night.
He is like a tree planted by
      streams of water,
   which yields its fruit in season
   and whose leaf does not wither.
Whatever he does prospers" (Ps. 1:1-3).

David advises us not to listen to the suggestions of the wicked, not to spend time with sinners or mockers, but to delight in God's revelation, and to meditate upon His words.

If it is my greatest desire to become like Jesus, I will not choose to linger long among those who have no interest in spiritual things except as I am ministering to their needs or telling them about Him. My choice of close friends will always be those who love Jesus just as I do.

"Then those who feared the Lord talked with each other, and the Lord listened and heard. A scroll of remembrance was written in his presence concerning those who feared the Lord and honored his name.

" 'They will be mine,' says the Lord Almighty, 'in the day when I make up my treasured possession. I will spare them, just as in compassion a man spares his son who serves him' " (Mal. 3:16, 17).

The apostle Paul talks more about this same need of Christian fellowship:

"Let us consider how we may spur one another on toward love and good deeds. Let us not give up meeting together, as some are in the habit of doing, but let us encourage one another—all the more as you see the Day approaching" (Heb. 10:24, 25).

Often I hear the voice of God speaking to me through the words of a Christian friend. Sometimes I find someone with whom my heart seems to knit together, as David said his did with Jonathan's. With them I can share my inmost thoughts, revealing what God is doing in my life. Their comments, suggestions, and stories from their own lives help to put what is happening in my life in perspective. No one should consider himself or herself infallible. Sometimes our reasoning may be carrying us away from the straight line of truth. A true Christian friend will help us find that out. The counsel of a number of Christian friends offers safety. They keep us in balance.

We all need a friend who will pray with us. I cherish the friends who enjoy praying with me, displaying no awkwardness or uneasiness. They are my best friends, for I know that they too hear the inward voice of God. With them I can shut out the world and turn my focus wholly toward Jesus.

Another way my husband and I have found to shut out the world and listen to God is through nature. The same God who created us to be His children, and who daily sustains us, is moment by moment active in the natural world. Although sin has marred God's perfect work in nature, much of God remains. The mysterious life that pervades animal and plant life comes from the same Being who gives us our own life. The heart that seeks God will find Him revealed in the things He created.

John and I both grew up in rural areas, and we find emotional and spiritual rest in the out-of-doors. Although most of our married life we have, of necessity, lived in the city, we have always sought times of rest and recreation in natural surroundings. When our children were little we used to go camping. As they grew into Pathfinder age we took the whole club for weekend backpacking trips. By the time our children reached adolescence we extended the trips to two-week summer excursions into the Sierra mountains with a church group. The memory of the world almost totally left us as we walked mountain trails, drank out of icy rivers, and set up our tents far from civilization. The basics of survival engrossed us: a flat place to camp, water nearby, a flat rock or log where we could set up our camp kitchen, a fire for warmth at night. The sounds and silences of nature blew away the worry and strain we had brought with us from the busy life in the city. We found a peace hard to achieve within the hustle and bustle of daily living and arrived at home at the end of two weeks refreshed and ready to tackle another year.

When John retired after 43 years in the ministry, we were able for the first time in our married life to choose where we wanted to live. We built a house on a mountain lot we had purchased 30 years ago. Over those 30 years we had often driven up the winding roads to our lot, parked and looked out over the valley far below, and dreamed of living here in the mountains permanently. Now our dream has come true. The plaintive call of the little mountain chickadee is usually the first sound that I hear each morning.

"Where are you? Where are you?" calls the chickadee, and my heart responds, "I'm here, I'm here, I'm not visiting, I live right here." Every day John and I thank God for the privilege of dwelling where the things we see and hear are the sights and sounds of God's creation. It's next best to living in heaven.

John and I long ago found that when we became involved with learning about wildlife, we enjoyed our excursions into nature much more. One spring I made an in-depth study of wildflowers, taking pictures, making a scrapbook, keeping a journal, learning the botanical names and families of each species. I have never enjoyed a spring so much! Our field trips were exciting. We visited the beach, studying coastal flowers; the desert, learning desert flowers; and the mountains, where color covered whole hillsides. As different flowers came in bloom we made several trips to each area. I assembled a photo collage of each area that still adorns our home, and my huge scrapbook is a treasure I will always cherish.

When we moved to the mountains two years ago, we were eager to find out not only what trees, bushes, and flowers grew in our area but also about the wildlife. The first night in our new house two raccoons tapped gently on the sliding glass doors hoping for a handout. Squirrels, chipmunks, and coyotes came calling within the next few days. But the most numerous visitors were the birds. Because I am nearsighted, birds have never especially attracted me. I can't get close enough to identify them, as I can flowers, and all I usually see is a blur. But because there were so many of them, we soon recognized the Stellar's jay, the scrub jay, and the acorn woodpecker.

The first winter we lived in the mountains we began to worry about how the birds found food to eat when snow covered the ground. When we discovered that many of our neighbors put out birdseed during the winter months, John made a feeder to fit on top of the railing on the deck outside the sliding glass doors of the dining room and filled it with birdseed. It created a lot of excitement both for the birds and for us! I could easily see the birds clearly that close at hand, and wanted to know, of course, just who they all were. As a result we bought bird books and binoculars and began learning. Now we watch for birds wherever we go. My binoculars are my second eyes.

That first spring in our mountain home a pair of Stellar's jays decided to build their nest on the underpinning of our upper deck. Evidently they had not read the bird book that plainly states that jays nest in conifers! But the birds had a difficult time building their nest. We get a strong afternoon breeze up our canyon, and every time they would have a nice pile of twigs on the board ready to fashion into a nest, the wind would blow the twigs to the floor of the deck below. My husband was forever sweeping up twigs. The mother jay became more and more distraught. It was obvious that she was anxious to get the nest finished so that she could lay her eggs. She clucked around like a broody hen as she searched for the spot where her nest was supposed to be.

"We've got to help those birds before she has a nervous breakdown," my husband said to me one day.

So we found a board that would fit on the underpinning, gathered up a pile of the twigs that had fallen from the location the jays had chosen, and John got out his glue gun. Together we fashioned a nest that could not blow away. I found some fiber-fill from my sewing room and lined the nest. John climbed the ladder and nailed the board to the very spot the jays had chosen, and we watched to see what would happen.

Mother jay seemed amazed to discover the completed nest. She fussed around over it for a couple of days, rearranging the top twigs and then settled down to housekeeping. She and Papa jay raised a family of fine young jays in the nest that John and I had built, never dreaming that anyone but themselves had worked on that nest.

I thought, *How like us. We think that we are in charge of our lives and never dream that God is the one who puts things together for us! Our plans and a little rearranging are only on the surface. God is the master designer of our lives.*

Filling our minds with the knowledge and wisdom that nature can teach us and steeping ourselves in the harmony of natural things closes the mind against the unnatural things of the world and opens a direct line to God.

Discipline of the mind—controlling the thoughts—is the key to learning to listen to the voice of God. Shutting out the voices of the world and tuning in the divine voice by thinking His thoughts may seem difficult at first, but the more we practice it, the easier it will become.

"All true obedience comes from the heart. It was heart work with Christ. And if we consent, He will so identify Himself with our thoughts and aims, so blend our hearts and minds into conformity to His will, that when obeying Him we shall be but carrying out our own impulses. The will, refined and sanctified, will find its highest delight in doing His service. When we know God as it is our privilege to know Him, our life will be a life of continual obedience. Through an appreciation of the character of Christ, through communion with God, sin will become hateful to us" *(The Desire of Ages,* p. 668).

Summary

It is God's plan that as we interrelate with Him and cultivate hearing His voice we become more and more able to control our minds.

In order to do this we need to *shut off as many of the voices of the world as possible:*

1. The inward voice of our carnal nature.

2. The numerous outward voices of the godless world.

God gives the born-again Christian the ability to *choose* what thoughts will fill his or her mind. We can choose to *shut off* self-pity, resentment, anger, or pride.

It is easier to control our thoughts when we shut off as many of the external voices of the world as possible by:

1. Limiting our time with secular magazines, books, TV programs.

2. Using God's heaven-ordained antidote for necessary forays into the world: the Scriptures.

3. Asking Him to give us a hiding place within our minds to protect us from influences around us that we cannot control.

4. Avoiding spending time with those who have no interest in spiritual things except to witness or serve them as Jesus would.

5. Choosing friends from those who love Jesus.

Christian friends are important:

1. They keep us in perspective and balance, prevent us from falling into error.

2. Often we can hear the voice of God through our Christian friends.

3. We grow by praying with our friends.

Nature is God's other book, and spending time in the outdoors can help shut off the babble of the world and open a door to hear God's voice.

CHAPTER FIFTEEN

When God
Uses Our Voices

*H*uman beings are naturally self-centered. We are more interested in ourselves than in anyone or anything else. The classic illustration of this is to pass out a group photograph and notice who each person looks for first. It takes us no time at all to find ourselves in it, does it?

The personal examination and inspection necessary to co-operate with God in the retraining of our minds might seem to turn us wholly inward. But the reverse is true if we keep looking upward to God rather than inward in self-pity. Honesty in accepting God's discipline will lead us to honesty with each other. Thus God will be able to use *our personal voices* to help others to know Him better.

One Sabbath after potluck I decided to pay a surprise visit to an elderly woman whom I visited weekly. Mae, a newly baptized Christian whom I had studied with before her baptism, decided that she would like to go along with me and meet Bea, the elderly woman. Furthermore, Mae's enthusiasm for the visit grew as she decided that we would take along a plate of food from our potluck for Bea and also two hymnals and sing for her! By now I had my doubts about the whole outing. I can carry a tune but am not blessed with a singing voice, and Mae's husky voice didn't make me think that we would be a welcome duet. But I surely didn't want to discourage Mae, so we set off in my car to make our visit. On the way I chatted about the ways the Lord was teaching me, relating a story about how God was disciplining me. Mae turned to me in astonishment.

"Do you mean that you still sin?" she asked in a stricken voice.

Quickly I glanced at her. Surely she was joking. But the horror on her face told me plainly that she was not.

I tried to explain to her that although a person was devoted to God, the Christian life was a continual walk, and God always had something new to show us about how we could serve Him better. I wasn't sure that Mae listened. It was obvious that she was disappointed in me. Here I was her pastor's wife, a leader in the church—and I still sinned.

I was chagrined as we arrived at Bea's house, sorry that I had let Mae down, embarrassed that I still sinned! Silently Mae got out of the car, and we went up to Bea's door. The woman was delighted with our visit, squealed over the plate of food—to Mae's enjoyment—and declared that we sounded like angels as we sang for her! Mae and I prayed with Bea and left in good spirits. But I didn't tell any more stories on the way home.

The incident left me a little confused. Maybe it wasn't a good idea to be so open about God's discipline in my life. But soon, of course, I was telling my stories right and left again, unable to keep quiet about God's work in my life.

Several months later in a small group at prayer meeting I shared what the Lord had been doing for me that week—how He had admonished me about something or other. Mae was in the group, along with several other women. One of the women, Ruthann, responded much as Mae had that other time.

"You're terrible, Carrol," Ruthann said.

No one spoke. I didn't know what to say. It was true, I was terrible, yet God loved me and was working in my life. But I wondered if He was telling me that it was time to quit sharing so much and so intimately. Maybe I was doing more harm than good by relating my experiences.

Then Mae spoke up on my behalf.

"No," Mae said, "Carrol isn't terrible. She's exactly like the rest of us, only she's more open and honest."

I realized right then that as Christians we must learn to be honest, to be willing to be misunderstood. If I led others to believe that I was perfect and never sinned, two things could happen, both disastrous. One, they'd catch on soon and know that I was deluded, destroying all of my influence for good. Or two, they would see sin in their own lives and be utterly discouraged because they couldn't seem to be as victorious as they thought I was. Much better to share my struggles with the other women and together pray for growth.

When we read in the Gospels about Jesus we begin to see God's plan for life on this earth. Everything that He received from His Father He gave to us. In fact, "there is nothing, save the selfish heart of man, that lives unto itself" *(The Desire of Ages,* p. 20). "In the light from Calvary it will be seen that the law of self-renouncing love is the law of life for earth and heaven" *(ibid.).* Everything in nature contributes to the life of something else.

As human beings we have nothing to offer until we receive it from God. And then it should be our delight to give it away. For by giving we find that we do not have less, but rather *more.* The world is filled with hungry, needy people—not necessarily hungry for food, but for comfort, recognition, and love. They need the comfort that God alone can give. It is God's plan that those who have received comfort from Him in turn pass it on to those in need around them. He wants to use our voices to reach out to the sorrowing around us.

One of my favorite verses is about this very subject: "Praise be to the God and Father of our Lord Jesus Christ, the Father of compassion and the God of all comfort, who comforts us in all our troubles, so that we can comfort those in any trouble with the comfort we ourselves have received from God" (2 Cor. 1:3, 4).

From personal experience I knew that it was true—God is the Father of compassion and the God of all comfort. When life overwhelmed me He comforted me.

I had spent my life in the church. My work had been in denominational circles as a pastor's wife and school librarian. My personal ministry had been within church women's ministries and youth and children's groups. Although I had often given Bible studies, they were almost always to those who had come to the church already interested in becoming Seventh-day Adventists. I knew little of the rest of the world.

When my husband changed pastorates at the same time our youngest child moved out on his own, I did not seek regular employment in our new city. Instead I looked for something that would bring in a few dollars and yet leave me time for writing and church work.

One of my hobbies is dolls. I decided to try opening a little doll shop in an antique mall. John and I found a space in a mall with an agreeable woman owner who was willing to allow my shop to be closed on Saturday while the rest of the mall was open. Since there was a cashier at the mall, I didn't have to stay at the shop, only keep it stocked with dolls. I picked up secondhand dolls that needed cleaning, hair care, and redressing, and delighted myself with their new birth. Soon I began attending doll shows and doll clubs. For the first time in my life I was involved with people who were not attending church, who were not looking to me for spiritual guidance. The topic of discussion was dolls—how would I find an opening to talk about the Lord? Someway, somehow, God always gave me unusual opportunities.

One of my new friends was Anita, the owner of the mall. She had three grown children—one daughter still at home, a married daughter, and a married son. Her husband, Ed, helped her at the mall whenever he was not working at his own glass shop.

Soon after I began dealing in dolls Anita left the mall for nearly a year. Her younger daughter, who often worked at the cash register and knew that John was a minister, told us confidentially that her mother was seriously ill and asked us to pray for her.

One day Anita was back at work again, looking great.

"Thanks for praying for me," she said. "God has worked a miracle for me." I learned that she and her father had both had cancer during her time out. Her father had died, but chemotherapy and prayer had apparently worked her cure.

Anita often played the organ at church on Sunday mornings while Ed, who made no profession of Christianity, watched the mall until she could get there. Anita and her daughters were greatly interested in spiritual things, and when they discovered that I had written a book about prayer, they insisted on having a copy as soon as it was published. Often they asked my husband and me to pray for friends and family members.

Then one day catastrophe struck again. Ed had not been feeling well, and when the doctor examined him, he discovered that the man had inoperable cancer of the lymph nodes in his neck. Quickly Ed began to lose weight and the future looked dark. But Anita was optimistic.

"Prayer worked for me," she said. "We'll just pray Ed through this, too."

And so we all began praying for Ed's healing. Anita took him for his radiation treatments and dealt with his physical weakness, refusing to let him give up.

One day when I arrived at the mall she met me at the door. "I have something to tell you," she said, urging me into a more private spot.

"This morning a woman came into the mall and bought a few things. I could tell that she was very distraught, so I encouraged her to talk," Anita said. "She told me that she was here in Loma Linda because her husband had been badly burned and was in the burn center of the hospital.

"She had come into the mall to try to take her mind off her problems," Anita continued, "but it wasn't working very well. So I just reached out and touched her hand and said, 'You'll just have to put it all in God's hands.' I told her about Ed and his cancer and what we are going through. I explained that it is God who keeps me strong.

"The woman was so appreciative that she thanked me and said that she believed that God had given me those words to speak to her. I told her that I'd pray for her husband, and she promised to pray for Ed.

"I do think God prompted me to speak to her," Anita told me intently.

I was excited. "Yes, yes," I exclaimed, "of course He did. Did you know that the Bible says that we will do exactly what you did for that woman?"

"What do you mean?" she asked, getting excited too.

"Wait right here," I said. "I'll go get my Bible from the glove compartment of my car and read it to you."

Rushing out to the car, I grabbed my Bible and hurried back into the store, opening to 2 Corinthians and that verse about the God of all comfort.

"Don't you see how you did just what it says we will do?" I asked her after I had read the verse to her. "Look, it says that 'we can comfort those in any trouble with the comfort we ourselves have received from God.' Because you are trusting God's comfort in your troubles, you could share that comfort with the woman who needed it so badly."

Anita beamed. "Tell me where that verse is so that I can find it in my Bible," she requested. I wrote the text down on a piece of paper, but then I began to worry that it might be so different in her King James Version from what it was in my New International Version that she would find it unrecognizable. (I really had no need for that worry. Looking the verse up in the KJV as soon as I got home, I found that it was very nearly the same.) Briefly I told her about the different versions and why I liked the NIV.

"I want a Bible just like yours," Anita said. "Where can I buy one?"

I told her where she could find a Christian bookstore and went on about my business. When I arrived home that evening I mentioned the experience to my husband.

"Why don't you go to the ABC and buy her a Bible as a gift?" he suggested. The idea thrilled me, for I love to shop for Bibles.

"Really, you won't mind if I do that?" I asked. "I don't want her to have just a little hardback Bible. It might cost quite a bit to buy her a leather Bible."

"That's all right. After all, we've never given her a nice gift. Go ahead and do it." So I did. I came home with an attractive leather-bound NIV.

My husband looked it over carefully.

"Why don't you have her name put on it in gold?" I gulped. Would wonders never cease? He was ready to spend more money!

"I'll take it back tomorrow and have them do it," I replied.

It so happened—I know that God planned it so—that the next day was the Friday before Mother's Day. I had Anita's name put on the Bible in gold and then had the ABC wrap it as a gift, taking it along with me when I went to the mall to put up my "Closed from sunset Friday to sunset Saturday" sign.

I handed Anita the package as she stood behind the desk. "This is a Mother's Day gift for you," I said.

"Why, thank you. I'll take it home and open it with my other gifts on Sunday morning."

One day early the next week I walked into the shop. Ed was sitting on a stool behind the counter, as he often did now that he was too weak to work in his glass shop. He had treated me like a long lost sister from the moment that I began my doll shop. Often he teased me unmercifully about my dolls, accused me of gaining weight—or whatever.

Today he greeted me with extra enthusiasm.

"Say, you really made a hit with your present for Anita. She doesn't usually get excited about presents, but she sure did about yours." He went on to say that the rest of the family had looked at the box and decided that it was a box of candy.

"No," Anita had said, "I don't think so."

"When she unwrapped your package," Ed told me, "she started jumping up and down and shouting, 'It's a Bible, it's a Bible just like Carrol's.'"

"Finally I got it away from her," Ed went on, "so that I could see it. 'Hey, did you notice that your name is on it in gold?' I asked her. She started screaming again. I've never seen her so happy over a gift."

When I saw Anita she thanked me for the Bible and told me how much she liked it. But her version of the unwrapping was much quieter than Ed's!

"Carrol," Anita said earnestly, "someday I want us to study

this Bible together." Yes, of course, I nodded. The unspoken agreement was that we would do that as soon as Ed was better.

Well, her husband didn't get better. Before long he entered the hospital. John and I visited and prayed with him often. Although Ed had not been a professing Christian, his wife and daughters led him to accept Jesus, and he began asking his daughters to pray for him. He seemed to appreciate our prayers, too.

One day when I was at the mall I reminded Anita that God doesn't heal everyone. Even good Christians die. "I know," she said. And the next day she asked me if my husband would have her husband's funeral.

Ed died the Saturday night before Father's Day. John and I arrived at the hospital just minutes after he was gone. We stood with the family and close friends around Ed's hospital bed while John read passages from the Scriptures about the resurrection and prayed for each of them. Then we talked about Ed and recounted stories of his relationship with each of us. All of us laughed and hugged a lot and cried a little. The Bible I had given Anita was in the hospital room, and she asked my husband to list all the texts that he read that evening on a blank page in the back so that she could read them over again. Later, on Wednesday, he read many of them again at the funeral.

"God gave you and John to our family for just this very time," Anita told me.

Although my husband, as a pastor, had often been intimately involved with death, it was a new experience for me. I had often attended funerals, of course, but I really had nothing to say to the sorrowing. But now, because I had suffered myself, I could comfort someone else. It was that verse of comfort being fulfilled all over again.

Not more than two weeks had passed by when Anita stopped me again in the mall.

"Isn't it time," she asked, "that we begin studying my Bible together?"

Anita set up the time and place for our Bible studies, and she invited two other Seventh-day Adventist friends, Bess and Lora, who also had shops in the mall, to join us. It was exciting to be a witness to Anita's spiritual growth from week to week. At first she was hesitant in praying aloud and offered simple and halting prayers. But as the weeks passed, her prayers became more fluent.

Eventually Anita's cancer returned. She sold the antique mall, and Lora and I began studying with her in her home. Anita's interest in heavenly things was refreshingly childlike. One morning as the three of us arose from our knees, she exclaimed in delight, "Didn't we all pray good prayers?" As we laughed at her candor, she went on, "Do you remember how hard it was for me to pray at first? But now I can talk to God just as though He were here in person with us!"

Because of her ill health we could not meet every week to study, but we got together as often as she was able to. Medication often clouded her mind, and she apologized for this. She knew that we were praying for her daily, and she trusted God. As the time came near for my husband and me to leave for a five-week summer vacation, I became concerned about what was going to happen to her. I feared that she would not live until we returned. Just before we left, I called her and agreed that we'd get together again as soon as we were home again. Our first week we spent at camp meeting. On Saturday night, as we were preparing to leave camp meeting to spend a week with one of our sons, we received a telephone call from Lora.

"Anita is in the hospital," the woman said, "and she is calling for you and John. She isn't expected to live more than a few days."

Changing our plans, we drove the 11 hours home on Sunday and went immediately to the hospital to see Anita.

"We're here, Anita," we told her. She smiled out of pain-glazed eyes. "So glad to see you, John and Carrol," she said. I spent several hours a day for the next few days just sitting beside her hospital bed. John came in when he could, and we prayed with her. She died on Friday morning. Yes, God had given John and me to that little family to walk through the valley of the shadow of death with them. And He had given them to us. He asked us to be His voices and His hands in ministry to that family.

Right after Ed's death and throughout the final days of Anita's life it seemed that I found suffering people everywhere to talk to. I read promises to heartbroken mothers of rebellious children in the middle of doll club meetings and wrote letters of condolence to those who had lost wives, husbands, or children. I waited by a hospital bed with a grieving wife and supported her through her husband's death and visited a friend who had just buried her mother.

"What's this all about, Lord?" I asked. I hadn't realized that there were so many grieving people around me.

The Lord led me to a very familiar verse:

> "The Sovereign Lord has given me
>   *an instructed tongue,*
>   *to know the word that sustains the*
>   *weary.*
> He wakens me morning by morning,
>   wakens my ear to listen like one
>   being taught" (Isa. 50:4).

"Didn't you know," God asked, "that when you spend time with Me in the morning I give you 'an instructed tongue, to know the word that sustains the weary'?"

The very same verse that God had fulfilled for me every morning for all these many years! That was the last part of the verse. I had not realized the responsibility that God was placing upon me to "sustain the weary" of the first part of the passage. Because I had turned to God for comfort in my personal problems, He was now able to give me an "instructed tongue." The comfort that God had given me I could now offer to others. Yes, God was able to use my voice to speak to those suffering.

No, the judgment experience—the retraining of our minds—will not make you reclusive or self-centered. It gives you God's words to share with others. Fellowship in suffering is a marvelous common denominator in any crowd. And genuine caring cannot be faked. Only the instructed tongue will truly comfort sorrowing hearts.

Summary

Cooperation with God in the retraining of our minds need not turn us inward in self-pity, but outward in comfort to the sorrowing.

If we accept God's comfort for our own sorrows, He promises that we will be able to comfort others in their troubles.

"Praise be to the God and Father of our Lord Jesus Christ, the Father of compassion and the God of all comfort, who comforts us in all our troubles, so that we can comfort those in any trouble with the comfort we ourselves have received from God" (2 Cor. 1:3, 4).

He promises to give us an "instructed tongue" to "sustain the weary."

> "The Sovereign Lord has given me
> an instructed tongue,
> to know the word that sustains the
> weary.
> He wakens me morning by morning,
> wakens my ear to listen like one
> being taught" (Isa. 50:4).

Fellowship in suffering will open doors and hearts.
God can use our voices to speak to those in need of comfort.

CHAPTER SIXTEEN

It's All
in the Relationship

I do not always have a strong emotional sense of God's presence in my life. Nor do I hear His inward voice in unmistakably clear tones every day. That is where faith comes in. By faith I can remember what I have heard Him say in the past and know that He never changes. I can read the Bible and by faith accept those words as His voice to me personally in the language of my heart. We cannot dictate to God just when it is important that we receive the delight of His inward voice in our impressions. God taught me that lesson the first week after I started the practice of sanctuary prayer.

When I began using the steps the priests took daily in their sanctuary work as a pattern for my daily morning prayer, God began retraining my mind in earnest. Oh, He had been at it ever since I had been born again in my youth. But I had so often complained and cried at His reproofs that it hampered the work greatly. But now since He realized that I was ready to listen and cooperate with Him, He began revealing the root sins that plagued me.

Although the disclosures were overwhelming, still I was excited to begin to understand just how God was working in my life. (Read *Practical Pointers to Personal Prayer* for the whole story.) I expected that God and I would be talking together constantly from that day forward.

The Sabbath of that first week I was disappointed not to hear His inward voice in my thoughts. He had been speaking to me so often throughout that week—why would He neglect me on Sabbath? It seemed to me that I should have a special blessing on the Sabbath. So just about sundown I knelt in my study and complained a bit.

"I can't understand why I haven't heard Your voice today, Lord," I said. "I'm disappointed that You haven't spoken to me today. Is there some sin in my life that I have not confessed that is blocking my ability to hear?" Receiving no answer, I concluded my prayer and arose to leave the room.

"Aslan is not a tame lion," a voice whispered in my ear.

I stopped in astonishment. The voice was so very quiet that I almost missed it. But I immediately knew what God was telling me.

C. S. Lewis, a well-known author of both adult and children's Christian literature, wrote a series of children's books called *The Chronicles of Narnia.* The seven volumes tell of the visits of children from our world to the mythical land of Narnia. Narnia, created perfect by Aslan, the lion, who represents Christ, has been taken over by the wicked witch, who has condemned the land to perpetual winter. The books unfold the plan of redemption as Aslan offers his life to pay for the treachery of one of the children. All through these books Aslan appears and reappears but only as he deems best. The land of Narnia has a saying that "Aslan is not a tame lion." In other words, one could not command or lead Aslan about. He alone knew when he should appear and when it was best that he stay hidden.

God knew that I was familiar with the story, and He took this way to show me that I was not to rely upon the inward voice of God in my impressions to keep me happy. No, I was to live by faith, and my faith must rest upon the Word of God. If I never heard His inward voice in my impressions again, it was enough that He spoke to me through the illumination of Scripture. Scripture is much more reliable than the senses.

I knew that I must share this experience with you before I ended this book. Some of you, reading my stories, might have concluded that if you do not hear His inward voice in your impressions, then you are not His child. Not so. Impressions may come from God, and they may not. Our trust in God must have its basis in faith in the Bible. The words of Scripture are our safest guide, and God illuminates them individually for us. That is why so much of this book is about the Word of God. Unless our relationship with God is firmly founded upon the Bible, it will never last when trials rush upon us.

A sense of the presence of God is not necessarily *feeling* His closeness—no, it is *knowing, by faith,* that He is near. It is true that often we will have a strong emotional response to His presence, but it is not always so. Then, *by faith,* we must remember the experiences of the past, knowing that "he who began a good work in you will carry it on to completion until the day of Christ Jesus" (Phil. 1:6).

It helps me to keep in a spiritual journal a record of the times and the ways God speaks to me. Then I can reread it to help build my faith. I believe that God daily speaks to each of His children. But we cannot designate in what way His voice will come to us. Whenever we long to hear His voice, we need only open the pages of the Bible and begin to read.

"The words of God are the wellsprings of life. As you seek unto those living springs you will, through the Holy Spirit, be brought into communion with Christ. Familiar truths will present themselves to your mind in a new aspect, texts of Scripture will burst upon you with a new meaning as a flash of light, you will see the relation of other truths to the work of redemption, and you will know that Christ is leading you, a divine Teacher is at your side" *(Thoughts From the Mount of Blessing,* p. 20).

Most often God speaks to us through the words of Scripture.

God has given us an added blessing in the writings of Ellen White. We should praise Him for the insights she brings us of the plan of redemption, especially on the life of Christ and the coming crisis at the close of earth's history. Her books, prayerfully read, studied, and underlined are a great blessing.

Ellen White tells us that "Christ's favorite theme was the paternal tenderness and abundant grace of God" *(Christ's Object Lessons,* p. 40). She says that it should be our theme, too. Referring to the inward voice of the Holy Spirit in our thoughts or as it opens up Scripture, she calls this voice "the inward illumination of the Holy Spirit" *(The Upward Look,* p. 155). In addition she emphasizes the importance of talking with Jesus:

"If we keep the Lord ever before us, allowing our hearts to go out in thanksgiving and praise to Him, we shall have a continual freshness in our religious life. Our prayers will take the form of a conversation with God as we would talk with a friend. He will speak His mysteries to us personally. Often there will come to us a sweet joyful sense of the presence of Jesus. Often our hearts will burn within us as He draws nigh to commune with us as He did with Enoch. When this is in truth the experience of the Christian, there is seen in his life a simplicity, a humility, meekness, and lowliness of heart, that show to all with whom he associates that he has been with Jesus and learned of Him" *(Christ's Object Lessons,* pp. 129, 130).

We can test ourselves in several different ways to know if we are truly walking in an intimate family relationship with God, and if the voice in our minds is God's. The apostle Paul tells us the Spirit of God will testify with our spirit that we are God's children (Rom. 8:16). This whole passage in Romans 8 is about sonship. Ellen White explains that the way the Spirit testifies or witnesses (KJV) with our spirit is through bringing us *joy.*

"This is the witness which it is the privilege of all to have—the joy of Christ in the soul through appropriating the Word of God . . . and bringing the requirements of Christ into the practical life" *(In Heavenly Places,* p. 144).

Listening to the voice of God always brings joy. Yes, even when it is in rebuke or discipline.

The *unity of the inward voice, the written word of God, and the conduct* is another test. God never tells us through our impressions anything not in accord with His written word. And if the experience of our hearts does not change our conduct, it is worth nothing. Unless our private time with Jesus leads us to be kinder and more considerate of others, we are fooling ourselves about a relationship with Jesus.

True religion begins in the home. Our parents, our husbands or wives, our children, will be the ones who can best tell if our relationship with God is genuine. Our coworkers in the office, those we deal with in our daily business—they will know if we really walk with God. True children of God will carry their own weight, not expecting others to shoulder their burdens. Not only that, but they will lift the burdens of others. They will be careful in detail, honest in even the little things.

Even the face will show that the Holy Spirit is resident in the person behind the face.

One late afternoon I stopped at the grocery store on my way home from work. Having a lot to accomplish that evening, I resented the time it took to shop, but I knew we must have the items. I searched for the shortest line at the checkout stand and stood impatiently in it. Mentally rehearsing the order in which to best get done the things I must do that evening, I did not see or hear the people around me. The man just in front of me was a joker. As he was regaling the checker with his funny stories, he caught a glimpse of my face.

"Lady," he addressed me, "don't you ever smile?"

Numbly I paid the checker for my groceries and left the store. As I got in the car I began praying, "Oh, Lord, forgive me for getting so wrapped up in accomplishing good things that I fail to be a true witness for You. May the expression on my face express Your peace and joy, not my inner anxiety."

I've never forgotten that man's query: "Lady, don't you ever smile?" The joy of the Lord should put a smile upon our faces. Even in repose we should look pleasant.

Once I took part in a Sabbath school panel discussion at my mother's church. Someone had asked me to participate just before Sabbath school began, and so as we filed out onto the platform I was still busily formulating what I was going to say. As the others spoke I was just getting my mind in focus. I shared a story as my part on the panel and felt that I had done all right. But later my mother commented to me, "The mouth of everyone else on the platform turned up, but yours turned down."

"Even when I was telling my story?" I asked in dismay.

"Oh, no, while you were speaking it was fine, but while you were just sitting up there you looked so stern."

I've been practicing turning the corners of my mouth up, cultivating a pleasant look upon my face even when I'm not smiling. Although I laugh a lot, I am also a very busy and intense person, and that shows on my face. I want to trust more in the Lord to help me accomplish all I have to do. Every day I pray, "Lord, make my face look like Yours."

God told me a few years ago that my name had been *Worry and Complaining* for far too long. He wants to give me a new name: *Trusting and Rejoicing.* It is not God's plan that I wait until heaven to receive my new name. No, He wants me to have it now.

"It is a very difficult thing for one to understand himself. We must examine ourselves closely to see if there is not something that must be laid aside, and then as we make an effort to put away self, our precious Saviour will give us the help we need that we may be overcomers" *(ibid.,* p. 145).

Our ability to hear the voice of God, either through Scripture or through the inward impressions in the mind, can get blocked in a number of ways. Willful sin, deliberately going ahead and doing what we know we should not do, will shut out the voice of God. It is impossible to appreciate Scripture when we are deliberately disobedient. Neglect of known duty will have the same effect.

Other ways that can interrupt the line of communication between us and God: busyness—allowing even good things to crowd out our time with God; worldly pleasures and friends; disbelief and doubts cherished; criticism and gossip; worry and complaining; neglect of church attendance; breaking of the Sabbath; failure to pay a faithful tithe; unforgiveness.

The wonderful thing about God as our Father is that if we face such a list as I have just enumerated, we need not work at checking the problems off the list one by one before we come to Him. No, instead we come to Him for forgiveness, and then He works with us to eliminate the list. How He loves us!

"The glory that rested upon Christ [at His baptism] is a pledge of the love of God for us. It tells us of the power of prayer—how the human voice may reach the ear of God, and our petitions find acceptance in the courts of heaven. By sin, earth was cut off from heaven, and alienated from its communion; but Jesus has connected it again with the sphere of glory. His love has encircled man, and reached the highest heaven. The light which fell from the open portals upon the head of our Saviour will fall upon us as we pray for help to resist temptation. The voice which spoke to Jesus says to every believing soul, This is My beloved child, in whom I am well pleased" *(The Desire of Ages,* p. 113).

John and I visited our son, Paul, his wife, Shery, and daughters, Cassandra and Mishaela, in the north woods of Washington two summers ago. Shery is a very healthful and good cook who prepares meals completely from basic natural foods. She has a full pantry of home-canned fruit and vegetables, a freezer filled with frozen berries, fruits, and vegetables, and bins of wheat and other grains. Paul raises a fantastic garden, and we feasted on home produce and delicious fruits and breads.

I remembered how many dishes and utensils it takes to cook for a family, plus guests, so whenever Shery began cooking a meal, I started the dishwater to try to keep up with the dishes she used in meal preparation.

One day after I filled the sink with dishwater and piled in the dirty dishes, I decided that it wouldn't hurt to let them soak while I set the table for dinner. I turned from my table setting as I heard a stool being dragged over the linoleum floor. Red-haired Mishaela, age 3, pulled the stool to the kitchen sink, climbed up on it, and industriously began washing the dishes. Her mother looked on dubiously, knowing that the dishes might not be as clean as desired and that the rinsewater was most surely cold. But Mishaela worked on, and soon the drainer was full and the sink empty.

I finished setting the table just in time to see the child swishing her hands gleefully through the empty dishwater and turning jubilantly to her mother.

"Look, Mommy," she cried, "I've washed them all. The sink is empty, and all the dishes are in the drainer. Look!"

"Why, Mishaela," Shery said, "I'm so proud of you for doing

the dishes. That was a big job, wasn't it?"

The girl's eyes sparkled, and she smiled lovingly. "Oh, Mommy, it's such fun to do the dishes when you're proud of me!"

I thought how much like that 3-year-old I am. Little Mishaela craved the approval of her mother. And I crave the approval of my Father, God. And when I hear His voice saying, "This is my beloved daughter; I am pleased with her," then all the trials, all the grief, is worth the effort. My work for my Father is not drudgery but fun.

It's all in the relationship.

Summary

We are not to rely upon the inward voice of God in our impressions to keep us happy.

Instead, we are to *live by faith based upon the Word of God.*

The words of Scripture are a safe guide, and God uses them individually with us.

Unless our relationship with God firmly rests upon the Bible, it will never last when trials come upon us.

Most often God speaks to us through the words of Scripture.

We should prayerfully read, study, and underline the books of Ellen White.

Ways we can test ourselves to know if we are walking in an intimate relationship with God, and if the voice in our minds is His voice:

1. Listening to the voice of God always brings joy.
2. There is unity between:
    a. the inward voice.
    b. the Written Word of God.
    c. conduct of the life.
3. True religion begins in the home: family members and coworkers can best tell if our relationship with God is genuine.
4. Even our face will reveal if we are a true Christian.

Things that can block out the voice of God in our minds: willful sin, neglect of known duty, being too busy to take time with God, worldly pleasures and friends, cherishing disbelief and doubts, criticism and gossip, worry and complaining, neglect of church attendance, Sabbathbreaking, failure to pay a faithful tithe, unforgiveness.

When our relationship with God is right and He approves of us, then all work for Him will be joy.

Also by Carrol Johnson Shewmake

Add more joy and meaning to your prayer life with *Practical Pointers to Personal Prayer.* Using her own deeply personal and triumphant experience, Carrol Johnson Shewmake guides you step by step toward satisfying communion with your heavenly Father. She tells how she lost the boredom and guilt that had choked her lifeline to God, and found intimate two-way conversation in its place. Paper, 128 pages. US$7.95, Cdn$11.55.

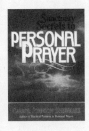

In *Sanctuary Secrets to Personal Prayer* Carrol Johnson Shewmake introduces you to a unique prayer experience that takes you through the steps performed by the priests in the Old Testament sanctuary. "If the daily work of the priests reveals how God cleanses each soul from defilement," she writes, "then following these steps in personal prayer can aid in cooperating with God." Paper, 92 pages. US$6.95, Cdn$10.10.